S0-ALK-628

Kicking Your Kid

Out
of
the Nest

Kicking Your Kid

Out
of
the Nest

*Raising Teenagers
for Life on Their Own*

Thom Black
with *Lynda Stephenson*

ZondervanPublishingHouse
Grand Rapids, Michigan

A Division of HarperCollinsPublishers

Kicking Your Kid Out of the Nest
Copyright © 1996 Thom Black

Requests for information should be addressed to:
Zondervan Publishing House
5300 Patterson Avenue, S.E.
Grand Rapids, MI 49530

Library of Congress Cataloging-in-Publication Data
Black, Thom.
     Kicking your kid out of the nest : raising teenagers for life on their
own / Thom Black with Lynda Stephenson.
        p.   cm.
     ISBN 0-310-20024-5 (softcover)
     1. Parent and teenager. 2. Adolescent psychology. 3. Teenagers.
4. Parenting. I. Stephenson, Lynda Rutledge. II. Title.
HQ799.15.B57   1995
649'.125—dc20   95-22426
                                             CIP

All Scripture quotations, unless otherwise noted, are taken from the HOLY
BIBLE: NEW INTERNATIONAL VERSION®. Copyright © 1973, 1978, 1984 by
International Bible Society. Used by permission of Zondervan Publishing
House. All rights reserved.

All rights reserved. No part of this publication may be reproduced, stored in
a retrieval system, or transmitted in any form or by any means—electronic,
mechanical, photocopy, recording, or any other—except by brief quotations
in printed reviews, without the prior permission of the publisher.

Designed and edited by Blue Water Ink

Cover and interior illustrations by Mary Chambers

Printed in the United States of America

95 96 97 98 99 00 01 / DH / 10 9 8 7 6 5 4 3 2 1

To Ken and Teresa Black—
my parents, who only and always encouraged me
to find my passion

To Art Miller—
a wise, old youngster who beckons us all
into the light

To Megan, Talia, and Joshua—
the joy of letting you go is dampened only
by the loneliness your mother and I will feel
when you leave our nest

To Debbie—
my wife, of whom I am proudest of all

Contents

Preface 9

Introduction **Fear** 11
When Children Get Big

1. **Letting Go** 19
A Simple, Fresh Idea

2. **Bursting a Bubble** 33
The Myths of Adolescence

3. **The Power of Passion** 51
Unlocking the Adult inside Your Child

4. **The Pain of Passion** 71
When a Good Thing Goes Bad

5. **The Parent Trap** 91
My Way or the Highway

6. **A Necessary Tension** 109
*Giving Up Control without
Losing Authority*

7. **Finding Your Voice** 129
*Taking Your Rightful Place
in Your Child's Life*

8. **My Kid Wants to Be**   *155*
        a Sidewalk Musician
        Helping Children Find Their Lifework

9. **Parents of the Future**   *179*
        Preparing Your Children for Life in the
        Twenty-first Century

Epilogue **Coming to the End of Yourself**   *197*

Preface

MY LIFE IS SIMPLE.

To love God, do good work, love my family, and be a good friend.

My precious friend and partner, Paul Lewis, has been a constant encouragement to me since we began working together in 1993. Paul's dream of Family University has provided a place for me to turn my work into play, and I love him for that.

My mentor, Art Miller, provides me with an ever-deepening sense of wisdom and an ever-widening appreciation for grace. He understands far better than I do everything in this book.

Lynda Stephenson continues to yank and tug and make something out of nothing.

Mary Chambers somehow finds time to share her love with her art, and Julie Link once again has made the whole thing resemble a book. My deepest thanks.

Sandy VanderZicht, thank you for taking care of me.

No one has invested more into this effort than Debbie, my wife. Twenty years together puts us into a select group. We are just discovering what it means to love each other.

Maybe I was wrong a few minutes ago.

Maybe my life isn't so simple.

I have teenagers in my home.

Memories of watching my son imitate me shaving are being replaced by those of him using my last good blade.

When did he actually grow whiskers?

And that can't really be my daughter, can it? Where did those curves come from?

Suddenly our home is a crazy, goofy, loud, wonderful place to live. But I wouldn't trade it for anything. This may be the best time of my life.

Introduction

Fear

When Children Get Big

Your beliefs will
be the light by
which you
see—but . . .
they will not be
a substitute for
seeing.

—FLANNERY O'CONNOR

 **OU ARE NOW OR SOON WILL BE** *(drum roll)* the parent of an adolescent. What word best describes your feelings on the subject? Is it *fear*? Not sure? Then how would you respond to the following?

Adolescence is a black hole waiting to suck in my child and there's nothing I can do to prevent it.

☐ TRUE   ☐ FALSE

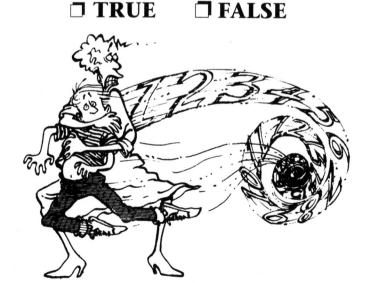

Admit it. You feel helpless to do anything to keep your child from falling into it, don't you?

Why? Because that's what you read about, hear about in church, and see happen to the teenagers belonging to your friends and relatives.

No matter how well we do for the first twelve or so years of our child's life, we believe a time will come when every young person will be swept away like Dorothy and Toto in the Kansas cyclone. And where they will land is anybody's guess. An entire childhood of parental influence will be gone with the wind, and the young person we find after the storm subsides will be a stranger to us until he or she reaches voting age.

So we hold our breath and watch for signs of change.

LIZ, fifteen, comes in the back door two hours late for dinner.

"Why didn't you call if you were going to be late?" her dad demands. "You know the rules."

"I just got a hamburger with my friends," she snaps.

"If your friends keep you from having dinner with your family, then you'll have to stop seeing them."

"You can't tell me who my friends are," Liz grunts as she disappears into her room.

WAYNE, sixteen, is sitting in front of the TV when his mom comes home from work.

"I thought I said no TV until homework is finished," she reminds him gently.

"I'll do it later," says Wayne as he continues to channel surf with the remote.

"What about your math test? You barely got a C on the last one."

"I'll study, all right? Get off my back."

BILLY, thirteen, is walking down the hallway after his shower.

"Did you brush your teeth, sweetheart?" his mom calls in the same sweet tone of voice she's used for years.

Billy glares. "When are you going to quit treating me like a baby?" he demands.

Fear.
It almost makes your hair stand up. **15**

Reckoning time is here. Your children are becoming adults and the only way you know to treat them is like children.

The old parenting skills don't work any more and you have no idea what to try next. Say the wrong word, demand the wrong thing, and that fragile little bird may take a nose dive right out of the nest. Or fly the coop forever.

You are smart enough to know that all the popular advice on the subject—hang in there, be firm, be gentle, give up— may not be right for your unique child.

So. What to do?

The one piece of information you are not getting may be the one you need the most:

The way we release children into adulthood is as important as the way we raise them.

Letting go is a process, not a single event, and once we learn to think of it this way our expectations will become more realistic and our response to changes in our children will be characterized by patience rather than panic.

Releasing children into adulthood is one of the final touches on the canvas of parenting. For some, these last few strokes are the easiest—they seem so natural—just like other stages of parenting come naturally to others. But given the right lessons and shown the proper perspective, nearly all parents can learn the finishing touches of letting go.

It'll be a challenge. Learning to parent an infant was much easier because he or she couldn't tell you what you were doing wrong, as your teenager no doubt loves to do.

But you can learn, and you can learn to do it in cooperation *with* your child.

Kenny Rogers wasn't referring to teenagers when he sang, "You've got to know when to hold 'em," but he could have been. And the writer of Ecclesiastes could have added another verse to his familiar thoughts on time. There is also "a time for holding on and a time for letting go." And those two extremes make up the mystery of adolescence. Up until now all you've had to know is how to hold on. But suddenly you have to learn not only *how* to let go, but also *when* to do it.

The ability to hold on to a child "just long enough" is one of the most important, though difficult, things a parent can learn. But it can be done. And it can be a time of fulfillment rather than loss. And yes, it can even be fun.

Our expectations for the "between years" ought to be positive. Our children are marvelously unique creatures, and launching them into adulthood is a reason for celebration, not fear.

So before you have a panic attack from listening to horror stories about adolescence, let's work on changing your expectations about what lies ahead. In the following pages you will find out how to . . .

➤ **Burst the myth of adolescence**

➤ **See your child as a young adult**

➤ **Develop your releasing technique**

➤ **Turn your child's life over to the child**

You have spent years nurturing the uniquenesses of your children. You have helped them strengthen and spread their wings. Now it's time to put those wings to the test.

It's time for you to let go.   **17**

Getting STARTED

#1 Put your child's name on a notebook which you can use as a journal to write your way through the experiences of letting your child go.

#2 Tiptoe into your child's room tonight after he or she is asleep. Remind yourself of how much you love this oversize person who also happens to be your child. Think about how loving an adult child is different from loving a young one.

#3 Take a deep breath and get ready for the roller-coaster ride of your parenting life. Your child has grown up.

Chapter One

Letting Go

A Simple, Fresh Idea

Every fresh discovery deepens the mystery.

—C. S. LEWIS

AN AXIOM OF LIFE SAYS THAT THE more you understand about something, the simpler you find it to be.

Keep that in mind, because the ideas that follow may sound too simple in light of all the complicated theories of adolescence whirling around out there.

So before we start, let's dump out the old, complex ideas, because simplicity, especially in this case, works. In fact, anything that's not simple probably won't work.

Unlike what many teach, the secret of raising healthy children is not in clever "control-them-at-all-costs" methods. Nor is it in . . .

❖ **Protecting them**

❖ **Sheltering them**

❖ **Beating them**

❖ **Taking them to church (sorry, but there are just as many screwed up kids coming out of church as any place else)**

❖ **Sending them to a military school**

❖ **Locking them in their room**

❖ **Your own clever (or last-resort) idea**

The secret of raising healthy children may boil down to this simple concept:

Your child needs to be released into adulthood while living in your home.

Knowing how and when to release your child is the key to good parenting.

This simple idea is rooted in the awareness that the outcome—the adult your child is becoming—is the whole point of childrearing. In other words, the means to the end should never be thought of as an end in and of itself.

It is surprising how many parents do not understand this truth. Many of them get lost in the clutter of messy rooms and forgotten homework and never find their way out. They try to solve today's family problems without any idea of where all of their efforts are leading. They forget simple truths about their child that can help them make sense out of all the chaos in their home.

As the old song says, we need to keep our "eyes on the prize." Parents need to be looking ahead at all times. Why?

Because the goal of every parent is to develop healthy adults, not to have a house full of obedient children.

After all, what have you accomplished if the three-year-old who sits quietly in church becomes a twenty-year-old who never darkens the door of one?

One thing is sure, kids don't come in a box with a picture on it that shows what they're supposed to look like when they are "finished."

Most models of successful families focus on the early years of childrearing. So how can we get where we want to be with our teenagers if we don't know where that is or what it looks like?

We need a goal—a clear-cut, well-shaped goal.

Surprisingly, we already have one. It's just so obvious that few of us see it.

The goal of parenting is to release well-balanced young adults into the world.

But wait, you say, isn't that putting the cart before the horse? Isn't that closing the gate after the cows are out? I want to know what I can do now to make sure I get the right kind of adult out of my teenager.

Your child was, and your teenager now is, an apprentice adult. And that is where we need to focus our attention.

Remember how important spelling tests seemed when your child was in second grade? How the world collapsed if he got a C? How upset you were when she was placed in the middle reading group instead of the top one? But nobody remembers them now without a conscious effort. And, even more important, NOBODY CARES.

What is your apprentice adult doing today that seems serious but won't matter at all in ten years?

At one time or another all children, because of their uniquenesses, act strange and silly. But behavior that seemed silly or strange in a child now seems positively absurd or unfathomable in a teenager.

Does that worry you?

Growing children are designed to have minds of their own and ways of doing things that differ from yours. This is hard to swallow for parents whose only focus has been on whether or not their kids were doing what they wanted them to do.

So what should you do the next time your teenager wants to do something you know (or think) is irresponsible, stupid, or unwise?

Instead of arguing, cajoling, or forbidding—take a deep breath, step back to a position of objectivity, and ask yourself the question that the rest of this book is going to help you answer:

At this moment should I consider my teenager a child or a young adult?

If you answer "child," there are already lots of books available, including *Born to Fly*, to offer advice. And you know from years of experience how to handle a fluttering child.

But if you answer "young adult," you are in a new and most uncomfortable situation. And that's why you need this book.

Letting a child make a decision you disagree with is one of the most difficult things a parent has to do, but it's the first and most important step in letting go.

Our son, Joshua, has an ability to start things. He has tremendous amounts of energy to get things going. But if the resources aren't available to finish the job quickly, he loses interest. He will stay with a project as long as he can see progress, but let things slow down and he's gone.

Several months ago, in a burst of energy, he decided that his dresser needed to be restained.

"That's a lot of work," I cautioned.

"I'm not afraid of work," he said as he took a drawer out of the dresser.

"That's not what I mean," I said. "I mean that the stripping alone will take hours. Then the sanding, staining, restaining, and varnishing will take even longer. I don't know if you really want to do all of that."

"Sure I do. It'll look better," he said, bending down to pick up his empty drawer. "I'll start on this."

Two months later I asked Josh to go out to the garage to get his one stripped drawer and put it back into his dresser.

How did I respond? Like any parent would. The dresser's one stainless drawer makes the whole thing look like a grin with a tooth missing. For a while the sight of it irritated me. But then I stepped back and looked at it from a more objective position and I saw everything differently. I realized that Josh

has to look at that dresser every day, too. And I know that it irritates him as much as it does me because quality is important to him. So that drawer does one very important thing: It reminds Josh not to start something that he may not have the energy to finish.

So now I love that grinning dresser because I know it teaches as it grins. And I grin back at it every time I walk past because I see it as a monument to one of the unique things about Josh himself.

25

Was it easy for me to let Josh strip one drawer of his dresser?

No!

Was it easy for me to go two months without saying anything about it so he would have a chance to finish the task he started?

Positively not!

Am I glad I did it?

Absolutely yes!

It's all part of letting go, the most important yet most difficult skill parents have to master. And it's a skill mastered only with practice—practice that should begin before our children become teenagers. If we don't start soon enough, we might . . .

❖ **Let them go too early**

❖ **Hold on to them too tightly**

❖ **Let them go too late**

❖ **Drop them from too high a height**

❖ **Never let them go at all**

In other words, the secret of good parenting is letting children go properly and at the right time. And letting go is a process that begins at birth and continues, in a sense, for as long as we live. For no matter how old we get, we will always see our offspring as children. And no matter how old they get, we will have the urge to interfere in their lives.

From the day our children are born, we need to be considering the time we will let them go.

For years, the day of letting go seemed like such a distant reality that the concept didn't affect how we went about our day-to-day lives. But then a day came when we sensed an unusual amount of restlessness in our household. One child was stretching those unique wings, and suddenly the house didn't seem big enough for the whole family. So we tightened our grip in an attempt to keep things calm. Before long, though, we felt wings beating against our fingers. We looked around uncomfortably because we were not sure what to do.

She wants out!
He wants to be free!
What should I do?

You have to let go. To prepare for the inevitable moment, here are seven release points to begin practicing today.

1.
Pay attention to your child.

YOUR child contains information essential to your success as a parent, and it is accessible in only one way: *by paying*   **27**

attention. How will you know when to begin letting go? What are the warning signs that all is not going well? How can you recognize the particularly important moments of your child's life? Only by being aware of what is happening in your home every day.

2.
Take responsibility for letting your child go.

LETTING your child go is not a spectator sport. It is your responsibility, not someone else's. Handing the responsibility to a youth worker, teacher, or other authority figure in your teenager's life is a mistake you will regret.

3.
Don't assume your child knows how to release himself or herself.

JUST because your good child turned into a good teenager doesn't mean you will sail through the releasing process. Remember, your goal is not to raise a good-looking, well-mannered kid. It is to deliver a healthy young adult to the waiting world. The verdict doesn't come in until kids are on their own.

4.
Don't impede or delay the releasing process unnecessarily.

LETTING your child go shouldn't take forever. You should complete most of it before your child is out of high school and all of it while he or she is still living under your roof. Otherwise you might be one of those parents who has a forty-year-old kid who has never grown up. And maybe never left home.

5.
Treat the reason, not the result.

DON'T become preoccupied with the day-to-day problems and realities of life. Keep one eye on the emerging adult. Look for the reasons troublesome things are happening and remember to keep the goal in view.

6.
Stretch your tolerance level to within an inch of breaking.

MANY teenage problems are due to parental intolerance. Don't rely on the "I'm the parent, that's why!" wild card. Such a stance creates more problems than it solves. Many teenage problems are due more to the zaniness of parents than to teenage rebellion. If you are never home to build a relationship with your children or if you react to them with knee-jerk responses, you may be the problem.

7.
Allow your child to make mistakes.

WHEN you let your child go, he or she will make bad decisions. Guaranteed. In fact, I still make bad decisions at

29

my ripe old age. And so do you. So expect some bumps and grinds along the way.

Have you ever watched a baby bird trying out its wings? As it plummets toward earth, beating its wings in futility, falling like a rock, you hold your breath. And then, just before you think it's going to splat on the ground, it grabs a bit of a breeze and somehow catches itself. And off it soars.

When you see that happen, don't stifle the urge to clap—for the baby bird, for mama and daddy bird, for your own apprentice adult, and even for yourself.

Before we get to the applause, however, we need to correct a big error in our thinking. All the good things we try to do will be undone unless we face two common misunderstandings that keep us from successfully letting our children go.

David's Story: Sixteen-year-old Ahead

DRIVING LESSONS

We weren't exactly caught by surprise. For nearly two years we had heard hourly reports of how many days were left until his sixteenth birthday. What surprised us was the pressure that seemed to build as we approached the date. He was expecting something big to happen when he turned sixteen. Having a driver's license, he seemed to think, was going to make a big change in our relationship.

But honestly, I was having a hard time figuring out what was going to change, and I knew he was going to be disappointed.

After all, he still didn't even pick up his clothes in his room. Did he think that all of a sudden I was going to let him take our car anyplace he wanted to go?

No way.

#4 Evaluate how your own parents let you go. Did they let you go too soon? Not soon enough? Maybe they still haven't let you go. How does this affect your ongoing relationship with your parents? With your spouse? With your children?

#5 How does the way your parents let you go affect the way you look at your own kids? Are you frightened of letting them go too soon? Have a good talk with your son or daughter about how your parents handled your teenage years.

Chapter Two

Bursting a Bubble

The Myths of Adolescence

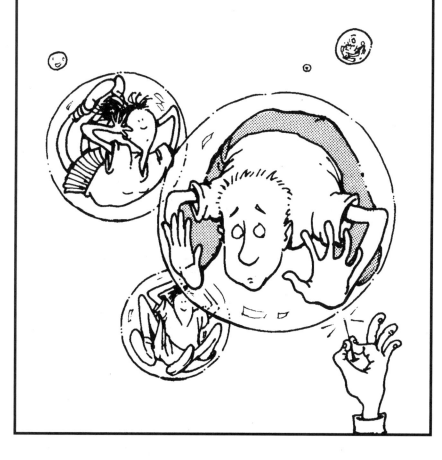

To be what we are and to become what we are capable of becoming is the only end of life.

—ROBERT LOUIS STEVENSON

ADOLESCENCE. Exactly what is it?

- ❏ **A freaky time of life brought on by raging hormones.**

- ❏ **The end of a beautiful relationship.**

- ❏ **Something that happens to every kid.**

- ❏ **None of the above.**

- ❏ **All of the above.**

You've heard the stories. Parents of teenagers seem to enjoy informing you that your happy days as a parent are about to end.

"You can't believe how bad it gets," a friend says. "My daughter won't listen to a word I say. Her room is a pigsty. Her schoolwork keeps getting worse. She talks back more and more, and I'm starting to worry about her new friends. She shows me no respect. It seemed to happen overnight. I can't figure out what went wrong. You just wait. You won't know what to do either."

You glance at your fifth grader playing quietly in the other room. She *did* talk back to you the other night. And that pile of clothes is still sitting on the floor of her room. Is this the beginning of the end? . . .

The stories about adolescence are so common that they have come to define our expectations. Ever since the word *teenager* was coined in the fifties, our expectations have been

35

shaped—both erroneously and dangerously—by such stories, as if they are scientifically verifiable, which they're not.

In fact, the stories you're hearing may as well be about the Loch Ness Monster, Bigfoot, UFOs, or Elvis sightings. They are bigger than life because people are talking about the *myths* of adolescence.

Myth, *n. a story containing an element of truth that is used to explain a natural phenomenon.*

Adolescence, *n. a transitional period between childhood and adulthood.*

Adolescence in and of itself is not a myth; it is a natural phenomenon in the life of every child. But it has grown to mythical proportions and gained a negative meaning as a result of our desire for some way to explain the troublesome behavior of some children in that transitional period.

This transition doesn't happen overnight, nor does it continue forever. (It just seems as if it does.) In our culture, it usually lasts from junior high through high school.

During this transition, two things happen . . .

1.

Your children begin to move about on their own.

ALL children, even young ones, exhibit a certain amount of independence. But when they hit adolescence they enter a period of time when it is appropriate for them to begin making their own decisions and taking responsibility for them. It is important for parents to allow kids to make these choices and also to allow them to experience the consequences, good or bad, with lessening degrees of interference.

BILL was a freshman when he tried out for the school play and won a part with a significant number of lines. Due to his difficulty with memorization and studying, however, he soon ran into trouble. Any encouragement from his parents he considered nagging. As rehearsals became more intense, Bill's stress level grew because he knew he was letting down the other cast members by not knowing his part. Finally, in anger and embarassment, Bill quit the cast and returned home crying, believing he would never again be chosen to do something he loved to do—act on a stage.

There had been a time when Bill's parents would have gotten involved in trying to work out the situation for their son, to the point of contacting teachers and directors personally. They realized, however, that this was a new phase in their son's development, so they treated him as they would a close friend who had gotten himself into the same type of situation. They made themselves available to help, but they didn't interfere.

2.

Your relationship with your child begins to change.

YOUR window of opportunity for establishing and affirming your child's values and character is closing. Your child's own uniquenesses and personal enthusiasm will become more and more dominant in the choices he or she makes. This will happen with or without your cooperation, but it works best when parents participate in the process. The release of parental control should be both intentional and gradual, and adolescence is the time when the process goes into high gear.

Like many adolescents, Bill wasn't open to parental influence until after he'd made a mess of things. Then, feeling defeated and discouraged, Bill finally opened up to his parents. They consoled him and talked through everything that had happened. Then the three of them put their heads together to determine what could be done to make something good out of a bad situation.

They came up with three objectives:

✔ **For Bill to learn more about his responsibility to others.**

✔ **For Bill to make amends in such a way that he might open the door for other opportunities to do what he loved.**

✔ **For Bill to accomplish this by himself.**

Bill's parents counseled him on how to apologize to the people in charge, and Bill followed through. He admitted to the director that his behavior had been wrong and explained the lessons he had learned from the experience. The director was impressed with the growth he saw in Bill and expressed his willingness to give him another chance.

In the process, Bill and his parents also came up with a way for Bill to overcome his distaste for private study. By recording his lines and listening to them over and over, Bill was able to memorize them.

The moral of the story is that Bill had reached the point in life where he had to take responsibility for his own actions. And, with the help of parents who changed their mode of parental operation, he did just that. The result was an outstanding growth opportunity for Bill, the apprentice adult, instead of a mess that the parents of Bill, the child, had to clean up.

The myths of adolescence have two sides. One side faces the parents and the other faces the child.

The Parent's Myth
Every child will become difficult to parent during the "between-age" years.

THE power of this myth is one of the reasons you bought this book. Right now your child is no problem at all. But you have been led to believe that things could go sideways at any minute, and you want to do everything in your power to prevent it. To hold on. To hold on to your kid. Because you know that any day your child may start to . . .

- Hate you
- Disobey you
- Lie to you
- Fight with you
- Embarrass you
- Make you wish you'd never had children
- Forget everything you taught
- Be out of your control
- Forget you

What kinds of unacceptable behavior am I expecting from my child when he or she reaches adolescence? What things am I doing that may cause this to happen rather than prevent it?

But there is also a flipside to this myth. Children enter these years with their own set of mythical stories.

The Child's Myth
"Nobody understands me."

THIS myth tells children that parents simply can't comprehend all the complexities of growing up, that parents still see them as children and always will.

And kids aren't the only ones who believe this. Many adults believe it as well. Think of all the professionals who are hired to work with this age group at churches and social agencies. Apparently we've been convinced that parents can't do **40** much with their own kids.

I am amazed at how many parents, simply because their belief in the legend is so strong, are willing to leave to someone else the critical act of letting a child go. Sometimes they even leave it up to their child or to their child's peers.

JAN was about to graduate from high school. She was a pretty good kid but had slowly drifted away from her single-parent mother and had established her own life with her own friends and her own interests. Jan's mother was beginning to feel as if her daughter were a stranger.

"I don't know how it happened," her mother complained. "We used to be so close. But then I couldn't spend as much time with her because of my job. Suddenly we were on different wavelengths, and I just gave up. What else could I do?"

"In the last three years, how many evenings have you spent alone with your daughter?" I asked.

"Alone? Just the two of us?" she asked me. "Why?"

"Never mind," I said softly. I already knew the problem.

Does your daughter think you don't understand her? Does your son think you haven't got a clue? Are they right? If all you know is the stuff they do wrong, maybe they're right. Maybe you don't know them.

Remember, understanding your child begins with understanding his or her unique abilities and strengths. That's where **41** the clues are hidden. If you know those abilities, you have the language in place to shatter the myths of adolescence in your own home. (See *Born to Fly* for more information.)

Where did the myth start?

IT'S hard to say how or why the myth got started. Perhaps some biological thing is going on. Maybe kids in the last few decades have become hormonally deranged. Or maybe it's behavioral. Perhaps parents over the past few generations have lost the knowledge of how to successfully release their offspring into the world of adulthood.

Whichever came first, the result is the same:

Children are leaving home as big kids rather than as young adults.

Although we can't be sure why the myth got started, I suspect it has more to do with behavioral changes in parents than with hormonal changes in teenagers.

And no matter where it started, it's pretty clear where it should end. Parents must take responsibility for *releasing* young adults, not just *controlling* them.

A parental pre-occupation with finding ways to control teenagers usually causes them to pull away rather than wait to be set free naturally. And children who yank themselves away or force their own release are doomed to a bumpy flight and maybe even a crash landing. And that's what we see happening all around us. In fact, that's what the myths are all about.

How the myths can hurt
The myths make you fearful.

FEARS caused by myths often result in reactions that can be devastating to your relationship with this "new creature" living in your home.

Nothing is more frightening to parents than to realize that a child in their home is suddenly turning into an adult right under their noses.

Wouldn't it be easier to ignore kids and let them figure out for themselves this growing up thing?

It might be. But only in the short term. It would be disastrous long term.

Yes, things are going on under your nose and all around that DO make you fearful. But how sad to allow a climate of fear to affect important decisions you have to make for and with that apprentice of yours. Remember, it's not unusual to be afraid. In fact, it's normal to fear things we don't understand. But it's dangerous to let fear control important decisions.

43

JIMMY was not just a good kid; he was a "great kid." In fact, everyone wanted to have a kid like Jimmy. When he was fifteen he was invited to a surprise party for a fellow band member, and he was excited about going.

"What time should we pick you up?" Jimmy's mom asked as her son put on his coat.

"I don't know, what do you think?"

His mom looked anxiously at her watch. The party wasn't starting until 8 o'clock. "How about 10:30?" she asked.

"Aw, Mom, the rest of the kids will stay until at least midnight. Can't I stay longer? I don't want to be the first one to leave."

"I really think 10:30 is late enough, Jimmy."

Years later Jimmy's mom admitted to me that fear made her tell Jimmy no that night. Although her son had never done one thing to make her question his behavior, she made a decision which implied that she did not trust him. She also admitted feeling sad that she had allowed fear to keep her from rewarding her son for being a responsible young adult.

But here is the really sad part. She also admitted that if the same situation presented itself that very evening, she would still demand that Jimmy be home by 10:30.

The myths of adolescence conceal the real agenda for these in-between years. Remember the goal: ***To release our children as young adults, not overgrown kids.***

The myths make you see your child as the enemy.

WHEN you see your child as an adversary, as someone with whom you are engaged in battle, you will look for

ways to maintain control rather than for ways to release your child. Your main weapons will be criticism and harshness. And when your weapons don't get the desired result, well . . . you know the rest of the story.

Children are not perfect. Far from it. And "almost-adults" may be even less so. But our goal is to grow children who can live on their own.

The myths make you hesitate.

THE myths of adolescence delay your releasing reflexes. After all, who wants to kick a child out of a nest and into a hurricane? If you hold on just a little longer, maybe the winds of adolescence will pass by and the atmosphere out there will be safer.

That's a tempting idea, but it's false.

Children who are not released in a timely and proper manner will play "catch-up" for years to come, trying to make up for their parents' missed opportunity.

Waiting "just a little longer" may be the worst mistake caused by the myths of adolescence. Just a little longer, a little longer, and a little longer. In fact, waiting may cause the very things you are trying to avoid.

What to do about the myths

S O, the cat is out of the bag. You know about the myths. Now what?

The rest of this book will show you a better way to look at adolescence and a better way to live through it with your teenager. In fact, you can start now to protect yourself from the subtle influences of these myths. Make the following a part of your new way of thinking:

1.

Don't believe the horror stories.

T ELL yourself (and believe it) that the horror stories associated with adolescence are exactly that: stories. Don't let other parents discourage or frighten you with stories about situations that may have been caused by their own mistakes.

2.

Tell your children that you don't believe the myths.

A SSURE them that you *do* understand them and that you are not afraid to know what they are thinking and feeling. Explain how difficult it is to keep yourself from being overprotective and controlling. Help them understand how hard it is to let go, but promise them that you are going to strive to do it the best you can, mistakes and all.

3.

Expect big things from your kids.

DON'T think for a moment that you are going to lose them to the "monster" of adolescence. See them for what they are—your one-of-a-kind children for just a little longer, on their way to becoming the one-of-a kind adults you have always envisioned. Then treat them with the respect any adult friend deserves. And continue to do just that. From now on.

4.

Take responsibility for releasing your child into adulthood.

NOTHING is foolproof. But most parents, when given a fresh understanding of these transitional years, become victors over the changing circumstances rather than victims of them. They are able to make the shift from a position of control over their children to a position of influence. And isn't that what you really want?

■ ■ ■ ■ ■ ■ ■ ■ ■ ■ ■

Sara's Story
Getting Ready to Drive

The thought of my daughter being out on her own behind the steering wheel of a car frightened me. Not that she couldn't handle it. It's just that there is so much to adjust and react to. I was worried about not being there to teach her.

So we arranged for her to take driving lessons as soon as she turned fifteen. That meant she was able to drive with us for almost a full year before she got her license. It was a bit of a pain sometimes, because her father and I made every effort to let her drive—no matter where we were going—so she could get the experience. It made some of our trips a little slower and sometimes a bit more dangerous than we'd like, but we were able to teach her how to control the car in the snow and how to stop in the rain and all the little things that may someday save her life—and maybe the life of a future grandchild.

Getting STARTED

#6 What is the biggest fear you have about your kid growing older? Talk to your child about it, and react to his or her response in your journal.

#7 Are you treating your teenager like a child or a young adult? Sometimes parents justify treating a teenager like a child by saying they haven't yet earned the privilege of being treated like an adult. But this can be a vicious cycle. Often teenagers contine to behave as children because that is the way they are treated by their parents. Someone has to break the cycle, and it will have to be you. Developing and maintaining respect for your child can be a challenge when misbehavior is involved, but every child needs and deserves it. Make sure you don't use lack of respect as a form of punishment.

#8 Find the good in your relationship with your child. Make it a point to tell friends and relatives about your young adult's positive qualities.

Chapter Three

The Power of Passion

Unlocking the Adult inside Your Child

A true painting
is full of the
spirit that
moved the
brush.

—GEORGE SAND,
letter to Gustave Flaubert

COLIN IS TWELVE. HE DOES NOTHING

but watch television and shuffle around as if he is in a fog. His parents don't like him to watch so much TV but they can't bring themselves to pull the plug.

"I just feel so bad for him," his mother says, shaking her head. "He has nothing to do. Nothing seems to interest him."

At school Colin just hangs on. Nothing interests him there either. Most kids call him a nerd. He hitches his pants up a little too high and never, not ever, has he been chosen to play keepaway during recess. He stands on the sidelines with his hands buried in his pockets and watches the other kids have fun.

What would you do?

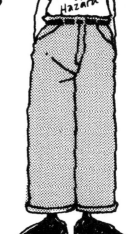

- ❑ Shake your head.

- ❑ Make the kids invite Colin to play their games.

- ❑ Give Colin a book on inspiring American heroes and make him read it.

- ❑ Have Colin tested for a psychological or developmental disorder.

Although Colin may seem to behave abnormally, there's really nothing wrong with him except a lack of self-understanding. And the lack of understanding is a problem lots of kids have. Your child probably has had or will have it at one time or another. In fact, many of us have it most of our lives.

The lack of self-understanding boils down to one thing . . .

The problem of passion

In a very real way, your child is lost. In the maze of homework assignments, household chores, rules for behavior, and a hundred other adult expectations, children lose sight of what they really enjoy. Some, like Colin, forget that they enjoy anything. And others, those who have always been reprimanded for doing what they enjoy, begin to believe that the energy propelling them has to be contained, controlled, and conquered.

Adolescence is a time when lots of kids get separated from who they are and what they were created to do because it's a time of fear for parents. A child who likes to play alone and doesn't need to be entertained every minute is described as "a perfect child." The same child as a teen, who likes to be alone, is described as "a loner" and is considered socially maladjusted.

The behavior didn't change, so why did the adjectives describing it change from positive to negative?

All parents want their kids to be perfect (and all parents have their own definition of what perfect is), but there is a larger issue involved than what parents want their kids to be; it's the matter of who their kids already are.

The biggest challenge of parenting is to help budding adults discover their potential, their purpose, and a well-suited plan for their lives. It's the challenge of helping young adults find where they belong.

Soon-to-be-adults are in a no-man's land of personal identity. They are no longer children but not yet adults. Many have lost their sense of direction, their sense of place and belonging.

To be designed for a purpose and to lose sight of that purpose is a sad thing.

But, you say, "My child has passion. Lots of it. If anything, there's too much emotion coming from that bubbling, boiling cauldron!"

Maybe yes, maybe no.

The problem of passion isn't that our children have none or have too much; it's that they don't know how or where to use the passion they have.

The common denominator in almost every story parents tell me has to do with their inability to understand, comprehend, or somehow get a grip on their child's innermost desires. Many parents even consider these desires a threat to their success as a parent. But they're not; they're really the key to it. When they're handled correctly, that is.

These natural abilities are, in fact, the fuel of life. And this fuel is so powerful that it can propel young adults to a place where they will serve their Creator and others with such joy, energy, and enthusiasm that they think they are serving themselves.

To get this fuel working for you and your child rather than against you, all you have to do is take the time to learn how to channel your child's passion.

The Release of Passion

Fortunately, Colin's principal understood the problem of passion. He had seen it many times before, and one of the pleasures of his work was identifying and channeling the passion of students who had gotten lost in the maze of growing up.

From his office window he had observed Colin standing around during recess. By questioning Colin's teachers, he found out that Colin was quite good at computer work, so good in fact that the computer teacher often asked Colin to do special assignments for her. So one day during recess the principal went outside to talk to Colin. He had a plan for releasing the passion he suspected was locked inside Colin.

"Hey, Colin," he said, placing his hand on the boy's shoulder, "I've got an idea. How would you like to come inside a few minutes early from recess and use my computer to publish the stats on the boys' keepaway game?"

Colin nodded. Then a glimmer of enthusiasm came into his eyes. In a matter of days, Colin had arranged all of the data in a way that gave up-to-the-minute stats on all the guys playing keepaway. He strode confidently out to the playground and handed out the data sheets to the boys as they came inside. Almost overnight, Colin became one of the most sought-after kids in the class. All the guys liked seeing their personal stats, but nobody but Colin could work a computer well enough to figure them out.

If you were Colin's parents, you would be kissing the principal's feet. And with good reason.

Discovering a child's passion is the beginning of finding the adult inside.

The Power of Passion

Which of the following are true?

❏ **My child is a moper.**

❏ **She shows interest in things I'd rather she didn't.**

❏ **He was interested in everything until he hit junior high.**

❏ **She has one overriding interest and is indifferent to all others.**

Whichever of these describes your budding adult, one thing is certain, passion is lurking in that sprouting body and expanding mind. A human being is a powerful force. And human beings (and the children in which they reside) are defined by their passion.

To understand this passion, there are five things you need to know. **57**

1.

Every child possesses natural passion.

THE problem is not that your child possesses no passion—or possesses the wrong passion. The fact is, your child has been designed with remarkable natural abilities that direct most of what he or she does.

Natural abilities, not acquired skills, describe a child's passion.

If you can describe your child's natural abilities, you will be able to describe your child's passion. And the ability to describe your child's passion is the beginning of communication. These natural abilities, this passion, is your key to unlocking for your child a life he or she can love.

How do you find your child's natural passion? Just ask.

My son, Joshua, tells me on the way home from school how much he enjoys leading a choral group in his high school. *Natural passion, I wonder?*

I pick up thirteen-year-old Talia from her friend's home. The minute the car door opens she begins to tell me how much she enjoyed helping her friend move her stuff to a downstairs bedroom. She especially liked taking charge of arranging the clothes in her friend's closet.

Natural passion, I ask myself?

Somewhere, hidden in the clutter of your child's life, are stories of passion. Stories of things he did because he *wanted* to do them. Stories of things she got involved in because she *enjoyed* doing them.

Listen for stories of passion

You never know when a story will come out. But they always do. They happen every day. You just have to listen for them—listen for expressions of enthusiasm, desire, interest. Listen for words that describe the thrill of doing something well.

Ask exactly what happened

Getting a teenager to talk is a problem for some parents. At first you may get only tidbits of the story, tiny clues as to the action and passion involved. Realize that the first time you

hear a story you are getting the condensed version. That's fine. Don't expect your child to offer details before he or she knows you are interested. So act interested. *Be* interested. Ask questions without prying. Be curious without being nosey. It's a fine line, but your love for your child is the balancing beam that will keep you from falling.

Work your conversation around

one question . . .

"What did you enjoy most?"

No tool is more useful for mining your child's passion than this critical question. These five little words release the mystery of purpose for your child. If you can remember to ask this question every time your child is enthusiastic about something, you will be amazed at the clear pattern of passion that emerges. You will begin to see your child's reason for living.

After asking Josh to tell me more about what was involved in leading his choral group, I asked him what he enjoyed most about it.

"I don't know," he said.

"Just think about it a minute. What was it about the experience that made it so much fun?"

"Well, I enjoyed getting every kid to participate and have fun. And I liked it because what we did was really good. Our performance was the best by far that anyone gave. I love it when it is excellent."

When Talia caught her breath after telling me about moving her friend's clothes, I asked her what was involved.

"I put all the clothes into their right place. I put all the sweaters together, all the pants together, all the shirts together.

Then I made sure all of them were turned right side out. Then I color coordinated everything."

"What did you enjoy the most? I asked.

"I liked the way it looked when it was done. Everything in order."

Pure passion.

Write down what you observe

Look for a pattern. Watch and listen for things that repeat themselves. Then write down your observations in a notebook. We all remember things better and make connections easier when we see them in writing. It is easier to see your child's passion emerge on paper than in your head.

(For more details about understanding your child's natural abilities see *Born To Fly*.)

2.
Forced behavior confuses the expression and understanding of natural passion.

WHAT makes the quest to discover our child's passion so difficult is how efficient we have become at getting our children to do what they DON'T want to do.

You know what I mean.

Many parents have well-developed strategies that revolve around bringing their child into continual submission.

The purpose of this book—if you haven't figured it out by now—is not to teach parents ways to get their kids to do what they want them to do (or to get them to *not* do what they don't want them to do); it's to help parents find out what their kids want (and need) to do.

The greatest pressure in most homes comes from parents who try to force the emerging adult into a particular mold.

A compliant child who generally does what adults expect may be hiding his or her passion for one reason or another—perhaps to avoid conflict, perhaps to avoid disappointing someone. Natural abilities tend to get buried when young adults are expected to do what the parent wants to have done rather than what they want to do. This is a parental glitch not a kid glitch, so it's one you can rectify.

Ask yourself these questions:

- ❏ Is it easier for me to describe what my child DOES do or DOESN'T do?

- ❏ How long has it been since I talked to my daughter in detail about something she enjoyed doing?

- ❏ Am I overwhelmed by the reality that my son wants to do things that are outside my comfort zone?

- ❏ Am I unable or unwilling to see the good side of what appears to be a difficult situation?

- ❏ In difficult situations do I focus more on my own fears or my child's opportunity to grow?

Were you honest? If so, you may feel a bit of anxiety. But hang in there. Once you begin to make sense of all that activity around you, once you can put a name to what your child does and how they do it and the natural passion that comes with it, the decisions you have to make out of your comfort zone get a little easier.

What mold are you trying to force your child into that he or she doesn't fit? What does your child do well that up until now you have seen only from a negative perspective? Use examples from real life that are positive. Describe them in a way that allows your child's true strengths to show.

3.
Few children discover their own passion.

YOUR child needs you. (Don't put your life on hold until he or she admits this, however.) Without parents, children have little chance of finding their way to the work and opportunities that will satisfy them for the rest of their lives.

If it were easy for people to discover the passion that steers them, a lot more adults would have lives and careers that are rich with personal satisfaction.

The fact of the matter is, personal passion is difficult to find simply because it's so natural—so natural in fact that the individual involved is seldom aware of it. It's like breathing. We're not aware of doing it unless someone points out that our chest is moving up and down (or puts a bag over our head so we *can't* do it).

Parents can save children years of lost time, lost energy, and lost happiness by helping them discover the passion that drives them.

You don't have much time to do it, however. In a matter of days, your son will leave home and your daughter will be gone forever. They will have begun a lifelong quest to find out why they are alive and what they are supposed to do.

Don't let them leave home without knowing their personal passion.

4.

Connect your child to his or her place of passion.

TO become a parent is to become involved in helping another person unravel two of life's great mysteries: Why am I here? and What is my purpose?

What an opportunity! What a privilege to assist another human being in self-discovery! Look at some of the questions young adults have waiting for them:

* *What college will I attend?*

* *Whom will I marry?*

* *What will I do for a living?*

* *Where will I live?*

* *What church will I attend?*

At no other time in a person's life do so many critically

important questions present themselves at once. How will your kids make their decisions?

It's not enough to . . .

* *pay for her college*

* *teach him manners*

* *keep her drug-free*

* *feed him*

* *buy her a car*

* *get him to do his homework*

* *make suggestions as to which careers pay the most or provide the most security*

The best guide for making good decisions is bound up within your child's passions. That which is good as well as that which could be harmful make sense when the language of passion is understood.

■ ■ ■ ■ ■ ■ ■ ■ ■ ■ ■ ■ ■

BILL is thinking about a career in accounting because he's been told that it pays well. But you have discovered over the years his natural desire to explore new things and learn how things work. Maybe a career in accounting isn't such a hot idea.

■ ■ ■ ■ ■ ■ ■ ■ ■ ■ ■ ■ ■

JAN is looking at a state college where the average size of freshman level classes is in the hundreds. You have noticed that Jan learns best when she is in very small groups and is able to stay focused on one class at a time, like in summer school. You suggest a smaller college in the midwest

65

that specializes in offering one course at a time. Your daughter is thrilled.

. . . .

HARRY chased a certain cheerleader for three years before she would even give him the time of day. Well, now they are dating and talking about the possibility of marriage. Will Harry still find her attractive twelve months after they are married when she is no longer running away from him? Maybe, maybe not. In any case, it's time to take your son out for a Coke and a heart-to-heart talk.

If you are able to set your fears aside and study your child objectively, you will be in a position to help your child answer these pivotal questions and answer them well.

And when you do answer, you may notice a funny feeling inside, because knowing that you are letting your new adult go in the direction of his or her natural abilities is to know that your child's chances for success, fulfillment, and happiness have multiplied because of all your work.

5.

Your joy as a parent is bound up in the passion of your child.

SOMEWHERE along the line parents have been duped into believing that our most important task is to teach children to behave properly. Yes, we must teach our children right from wrong, bad from good, this from that, in everything from brushing their teeth to not burping at the table. Yes, our days are filled with such mundane responsibilities. But when we get past the do's and don'ts of life and begin to guide our children into discovering and nurturing and releasing the abilities God gave them, we find out what true joy is. And there is no greater joy for parents than seeing their children filled with joy.

Ted is a businessman in his late fifties whose daughter just graduated from college.

"She got a job directing the symphony in Nashville," he told me proudly.

"Is she happy?" I asked.

"You bet," Ted nodded. "It's what she has always wanted to do."

I leaned over and looked him in the eye. "That's wonderful! How do you feel about it?"

Ted sighed and looked down for a moment. When he looked up, his eyes were full of tears. "I have never been more happy about anything in my life," he whispered.

The Starting Line

See that kid in the other room? The one who is starting to shave. The one who leaves the toilet seat up and hates doing homework and wouldn't hang up his clothes if his life depended on it.

He is so special to you that thinking about his happiness almost makes your stomach hurt, doesn't it? And one day, if it hasn't happened already, his joy will be one of the most important things in your life. And his joy—and yours—is connected to his passion.

Is it worth the trouble of figuring out what that passion is?

DRIVING LESSONS

Sara's Story
Freedom

It's gotten almost goofy around the house the last few years. With four kids between the ages of ten and sixteen, it seems as if all my husband and I do is drive the kids around to where they need to go. It irritates me when other moms say that we do too much for our kids. We don't. It's just that the cumulative effect is overwhelming. One Saturday last month I counted nineteen trips to take the kids places and pick them up again.

So when my daughter got her license last month, the first thing I thought was that we'd both have some freedom. She would be free to live her life according to her plans without me to cart her around. And, just as important, I would be free. I didn't see her as such a responsibility anymore. Almost overnight she seemed more like an adult friend, making her own decisions about when and where she is going. I almost don't know how to relate to her with this new freedom. Is she a child or an adult?

#9 Talk to your child about something he or she enjoyed doing—either at school or at home, either with friends or alone. Talk until you figure out what was so enjoyable about it. Write about it in your journal.

#10 Does your child's passion resemble yours or is it different? Does your child know what you are passionate about? Talk about your passion with each of your children.

#11 If you are thinking that your greatest joy will come when your child moves out of the house, you don't get it. Stretch yourself to imagine how fulfilling it would be to have a strong, vital relationship with your adult child and how satisfying it would be to know that you helped your child find, develop, and pursue the passion of his or her heart.

Chapter Four

The Pain of Passion

When a Good Thing Goes Bad

So many die
before they
awaken.

—SUFI SAYING

THERE IS A FIRE IN THE BELLY OF your child. You've noticed it. We've talked about it. Your child's abilities are wonderful, but they have a down side . . .

The natural abilities your child uses so well have been given *without restraints.*

And therein lies a danger.

Passion Consumes

Consume, *v., to take over completely; to destroy.*

Young adults are designed to soar on wings of passion and enthusiasm. But the very passion that keeps them in the air also puts them in great danger.

So the best we have to say about your child may also be the worst. Too much of a good thing can be bad . . . if you don't know what to watch for.

Parents assume that the greatest danger their children face when they enter the outside world is in the things they do poorly—like math or car repair or assertiveness. But the reality **73** is that we all learn early to compensate for things we don't do well or can't do; yet we never think to watch out for the things that we are good at doing.

So while much parental attention is directed toward what a child *doesn't* do well, the young adult is in danger of being consumed by the very thing that he or she *does* do well.

Do these stories sound familiar?

JENNY has a natural ability to work on her own with little or no outside direction. She does her best work when she is calling the shots and no one is telling her what to do. Now that she's older, her parents are finding her more difficult to get along with when they try to influence her decisions. She actually seems to push them away, which hurts their feelings and makes them angry.

. . . .

JOHN has a natural ability to get people to respond to him. He is a sophomore and a girl at school has caught his eye. It's his first attempt at having a girlfriend and he wants to send her flowers even though he's not yet taken her on a date. He's not too happy when his dad cautions him against doing something that will draw a strong response from the girl before he even knows what she is like.

. . . .

SALLY has a natural ability to interact with others, and she is spending more and more time with her friends. Her homework is beginning to suffer as a result, but when her parents question her about it, they feel as if they have stepped in front of a moving freight train.

JENNY. JOHN. SALLY. Their strengths are also their weaknesses.

Odd, isn't it? The very thing they are good at doing has the potential to be bad for them.

How has this been true in your own life? Think about some of the things you have gotten into trouble for over the years. Do you see a connection between those things and the good things you do?

Your young adult is, for the first time, in a position to do something to satisfy the needs and desires he or she feels. And their ever-increasing sense of passion makes adolescents feel powerful. And indeed they are. The energy packed inside your child has enormous potential for good, if you can just keep it from blowing up at the wrong time or in the wrong place.

Passion Blinds

At seventeen, Jenny is so self-sufficient that she can't imagine a time when she will ever need anyone to help her with anything. And she's never had to ask for advice; she always seems to know exactly what needs to be done or said in every situation. Her abilities have blinded her to the possibility that she may yet encounter situations that call for more knowledge and wisdom than she has been blessed with naturally. Her natural abilities also make her impatient with people who

75

aren't like her, especially those who don't hesitate to ask for help and guidance. She considers them weak and stupid.

Although Jenny has a high level of natural wisdom, she is totally ignorant of certain realities.

The only thing Jenny sees is what needs to be done, and she sets about doing it in the most efficient way possible, oblivious to the needs of other people as well as to how her behavior affects others.

And when her parents try to point out this obvious blind spot Jenny becomes indignant.

Passion burns up discernment

John is confused. His parents have always taught him that he should be kind, generous, and thoughtful, but now his dad is trying to discourage him from doing exactly that. All he wants to do is buy flowers for a girl at school. *What's the big deal?* he wonders. And why is his dad suddenly changing his own rules? What could possibly be wrong with doing something nice for someone? The only logical explanation John can come up with for this odd behavior is that his father is inconsistent. And he tells him so. John's passion to get a response is so strong that he is unable to discern potential harm in anything he wants to do.

Apprentice adults are at a definite disadvantage. They are being consumed and directed by intense and overwhelming natural passion, which tells them what to do and how to do it—and it feels so right!

Passion determines priorities

Sally doesn't understand what the problem is. She just wants to spend time with her friends. That's all. She'll squeeze

her homework in when she has time. *What's wrong with doing what I want to do?* she wants to know.

Usually nothing. But when it gets in the way of important priorities, the passion needs to be managed. Because unleashed passion is a powerful force.

So what do our apprentice adults say when parents point out the potential problems in their actions?

JENNY: *"Mom, just get off my back! I can make my own decisions."*

JOHN: *"Dad, it won't hurt anything to give her flowers. It's no big deal."*

SALLY: *"I want to be with my friends. I'll get my homework done. Don't worry about it."*

77

They just don't get it. But it shouldn't be any surprise. Most adults don't get it either. Why do you think so many of us crash and burn as we move through our grown-up years? Because we have never learned how our own personal passion consumes and blinds *us*.

What is your personal passion? In what areas does it blind you? How does it affect the way you see your child? How has it affected your discernment and your priorities?

The pain of passion

Natural passion is the energy that drives your child, but energy out of control can cause lots of pain, even death.

The unrestrained passion of natural abilities is the greatest threat to a healthy adult life.

To keep your child from becoming a victim of his or her own passion, here are four prescriptions.

1.

Allow your child to learn from poor decisions.

NOT every poor decision is a wrong decision. Most of life is lived in the gray areas where right and wrong are not clearly defined. In those situations, a number of alternatives may be equally valid. This is where knowledge, wisdom, and passion come into play. This is where everything your child has learned intersects with all that he or she believes and feels.

Making poor decisions and suffering the consequences is how we all learn to manage our passions. But this learning has to be done in situations that fall into life's gray areas.

Unfortunately, it is not always easy for parents and teenagers to agree about what is gray.

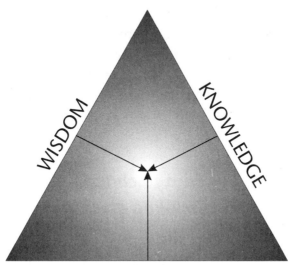

The best decisions are those that take into account all the wisdom, knowledge, and passion that we possess.

After all, you have your own natural passions, which, over the years, have solidified into strong opinions. You have ways of doing things that work well for you, and it's hard for you to accept that your ways may not be the best ways for your child.

So whose ways take precedence and why? Who calls the shots in what areas? Who makes decisions when the matter in question does not involve a black and white issue? How do you know whether your child's seemingly poor decision is one that he or she should be allowed to learn from or one that should be intercepted and changed?

The next time you are talking with your child and you feel compelled to give input, ask yourself . . .

Is there an absolute moral right or wrong in this situation?

If not, ask . . .

* *What would my own passion lead me to do?*

* *What passion or natural ability is driving my child?*

Some decisions are flat out wrong (e.g., to lie, steal, cheat). So when a child's natural abilities become so strong that he or she makes a decision that is morally wrong, parents need to be prepared to administer the appropriate discipline.

2.
Learn to change from a discipline-giver to a direction-giver.

MAKE this change a personal goal. Sometime during the years of trans-

formation you are going to have to bite the bullet and change the way you relate to your apprentice adult. The rules and guidelines you've been living by no longer fit your relationship.

Once children reach the "'tween-age" years, they are quite busy arranging and re-arranging their lives to accommodate their personal passions. So, while discipline may have been effective for enforcing obedience when they were younger, you are discovering that discipline alone is no longer the answer. In fact, your attempts at discipline are about as effective as trying to redirect a hurricane with an electric fan. The more important issue now is to help your children learn to manage their natural passion without being consumed by it.

The difference is *direction* versus *discipline*. In many ways this difference is subtle. Life doesn't slice itself into nice even pieces, and many times matters of discipline and direction overlap. When family life fills up with scenes of communication confusion, slammed doors, and shouting matches, what is called for is *discipline through direction*. Here are a few suggestions to help you learn this new skill.

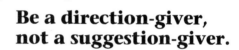

Be a direction-giver, not a suggestion-giver.

Joshua had a big paper due in three days, which was two days before he would ordinarily start on it. Joshua works best against a deadline and usually does his finest work at the last minute, so Debbie and I try not to get uptight when he puts things off. However, one look at our calendar told me that the next two nights were not available to Joshua. Family commitments would keep all of us away from home both nights.

At sixteen, Joshua was getting too old for me to hammer on him about his homework. So I tried the indirect approach. **81**

"When are you going to do your paper?" I asked.

"Thursday night," he replied casually.

"We won't be home."

"Then I'll figure out something else."

"Come over here and sit down a minute," I said.

I knew he was feeling uncomfortable, but I was determined to make him think about his decision, even though I had no intention of taking it away from him.

"Let's think out loud a minute," I said. "You can't really do it Thursday night. You won't be home. And you can't do it Wednesday night. You won't be home. The only time you have is right now.

"But I don't want to do it now. I don't have the energy. It's late and I want to go to bed."

"Your choice," I said, getting up from my chair. "But if you want to work on it now, I'll sit up with you and read and make us some popcorn."

Ten minutes later I came back through the living room and found Josh working on his paper. I turned around and went to make popcorn.

Becoming a direction-giver means much more than offering a few half-hearted suggestions to your teenager. A significant responsibility comes with this new phase of the relationship. Obedience alone is no longer enough. You now need understanding as well. That's right. You need to take the time to make sure your teenager not only *hears* you, but *understands* you as well. For this to happen, make gentle forcefulness a part of your communication style.

Don't give directions without taking time to talk.

Thirteen year-old Jackie was mad at one of her friends. The friend had lied about her, and Jackie was furious. Her mother cautioned her against calling her friend while she was mad. "You may say something you'll regret," she warned. But Jackie made the call anyway and, just as her mother had predicted, got herself into more of a mess than ever.

"What could I have done differently?" Jackie's mother asked me. "I know I was forceful. We stood by the phone and argued for several minutes."

I offered her the same tip I'm offering you: Don't give directions without taking time to talk.

If at all possible, find a place to sit down. Even the brief time it takes to pull out a dining room chair or find a place in the mall is often enough to allow some of the anger and hostility to subside.

Remain calm. Doing so will force the escalating situation to de-escalate. Only then will you have any hope of getting your point across. Hysterical teenagers have ears that serve only one purpose: they hold their earrings.

I'm not suggesting that all young adults can be talked into agreeing with their parents all the time. But I am saying that we need to work at making sure our children understand *how* we think, not just *what* we think. And they need to know *why* we feel so strongly about particular issues. If we are unable to articulate our convictions or concerns, perhaps we need to reconsider them ourselves.

How would I need to speak to you if I wanted you to reconsider a decision you were making? Which of the following are most likely to get a positive response from you?

❑ **Call you stupid.**

❑ **Threaten you within an inch of your life.**

❑ **Make it clear that your way is flat-out wrong, no exceptions.**

❑ **Make sure you feel my disapproval and disappointment if you disagree with me.**

❑ **Raise my voice in pitch and decibel level.**

❑ **Listen to your opinion.**

❑ **Sit down with you and exchange viewpoints.**

And depending upon how serious the potential pain might be, shouldn't I . . .

❑ **Make time to talk through the issue with you?**

❑ **Allow you to make your decision and experience the consequences?**

For the next several years your kid is going to live in the pain of his or her passion (and so are you). Some of the things you point out will go unheeded simply because teenagers have tremendous energy to do things "their way." And yet—in the end—the lessons you teach your child, whether few or many, will last a lifetime.

3.

Preserve their passion while changing their direction.

JOHN is fourteen, and he loves to figure things out. His mom bought a new bench for the living room, and it was delivered unassembled in a box. John wasn't home from school for ten minutes before he had the box open and all the pieces strewn across the living room floor.

This did not please his mother. However, rather than lose her temper and destroy her son's initiative she remained calm.

"Johnny," she said, "I appreciate your wanting to help put this together, and I know you love to figure things out, but I think we need to read the instructions first. So I want you to put all the pieces back in the box and wait until we have time to sit down, read the instructions, and make sure all the pieces are here. Then you can help put it together."

Underneath every poor decision is one truth: Your child has a passion for doing things a particular way.

Your initial response to a raging adolescent might be to get out of the way and stay out of the way. But emerging adults need parents who continue to offer advice, even though they reject more of it than they take.

Remember, apprentice adults do not fully understand who they are or what they do. Helping children identify, understand,

85

and control their own passion before they are consumed by it is one of the ultimate joys of parenthood.

4.

Know your two options when headed for pain.

DIRECTION-giving parents avoid using power to manipulate children into their own comfort zone. As their children get older, these parents learn self-restraint. They limit themselves to making only those decisions that require their direction. But what do they do when their child's passion is about to cause pain?

They have two options:

Option 1: *Adjust direction.*

JEFF worked hard all weekend on a lawn job and earned fifty dollars. Jeff's natural abilities to acquire things caused him to begin looking through newspapers for something to buy. Seeing what was happening, his dad sat down with him and reminded him of his tendency to acquire things he doesn't need. Then he suggested that Jeff buy a couple smaller things to satisfy his desire. (After all, he had worked hard all weekend, and it wasn't morally wrong to spend some of his money.) Jeff agreed with his dad and spent twenty dollars instead of fifty and saved the rest.

Through quiet counsel Jeff's dad adjusted his son's direction and spared him the pain of waking up the next day and being depressed because he had blown all of his money. And the best part: Jeff understood WHY his first instincts were to spend all his money. His father had helped him adjust direction *and* preserve his passion.

Option 2: *Change direction.*

STACEY had a history of making poor decisions about friends. Her desire to interact and unite with other people had made her vulnerable to relationships with kids who did things that were not only bad but illegal. She continually ignored all advice, warnings, and direction from her parents and refused to take responsibility for herself.

Having exhausted every option they knew, Stacey's parents sold their house and moved the entire family to a community thirty miles away where Stacey could make a fresh start.

Wow.

Parents have to work extra hard when their emerging adult is about to make a decision that is flat wrong. When passion pushes an adolescent toward a decision with dire consequences, it is the right and obligation of parents to step in and change the child's direction.

Doing so may not win them any popularity contests, but it may preserve their relationship.

Every stage of a child's life involves uncomfortable situations. Only one thing is more uncomfortable than allowing a child to make decisions that are different from those you would make: standing by while a young adult makes *poor* decisions.

But that is what it means to be a parent . . .

❏ It means knowing when to step in and when to step aside.

❏ It means knowing when to allow passion to have its full expression and when to channel it in some other direction.

❏ It means knowing the difference between a poor decision and a bad decision.

❏ It means having the courage to allow a child to suffer the consequences of a *poor* decision and having the courage to step in to prevent a *bad* decision.

❏ It means suffering with them the consequences of poor decisions.

But it also means sharing with them the joy of good decisions. Being there for both—damage control *and* praise—make you a great parent.

■ ■ ■ ■ ■ ■ ■ ■ ■ ■ ■ ■ ■

Sara's Story
Handing Her My Life

DRIVING LESSONS

The strangest feeling came over me the first time I rode in the passenger seat of our car as my daughter drove down the road at fifty miles an hour. Never before had my life been in her hands. It had always been the other way around. I've always been the protector. It's wasn't that I didn't trust her. It was more like being seen naked. I was so used to telling her what to do that I found myself biting a hole in my lip to keep from screaming. One mistake could kill us both. I felt very vulnerable and exposed and, well, surprised. I acted as if everything was fine. But I didn't feel that way. And still don't. At least not yet.

Getting STARTED

#12   Is your child out of control? Can you trace the behavior to natural abilities that are steering his or her passion? Note in your journal your child's two or three abilities that you think are also his or her greatest threat.

#13   Which of your child's misguided passions is the most difficult for you to accept? Can you figure out why? Write about it in your journal.

#14   The next time your child is out of step, begin your talk with him or her by identifying the strength you see that needs to be controled. Note how this simple maneuver changes the direction of your conversation.

Chapter Five

The Parent Trap

My Way or the Highway

People have
one thing in
common—they
are all different.

—ROBERT ZEND

IMAGINE FOR A MOMENT THAT YOU'RE not a mom or a dad. How would your day be different if you could make decisions without regard to your children? ***Would you . . .***

- ❏ hop out of bed or sleep in?
- ❏ pig out on ice cream or prepare a meal of herbs and sprouts?
- ❏ go to the movies or to the health club?
- ❏ clean the whole house superficially or clean one room thoroughly?
- ❏ finish that book you've started three times or go skiing?
- ❏ sit on the porch alone and look at the stars or invite friends to join you?

Remember when you . . .

❏ did things your own way?

❏ ate what tasted good to you?

❏ took a nap if you were exhausted?

❏ listened to music that had words you could understand?

❏ stayed home if you didn't feel like going out?

❏ went out if you didn't feel like staying home?

❏ used the car without first checking with your teenager?

Can you remember a time when what YOU wanted to do and the way you wanted to have it done was all that mattered to you? Are you still like that? If so, beware. This kind of thinking is a trap. And it can keep your young-adult-in-training from developing his or her own natural ways of doing things.

THE PARENT TRAP

There is nothing unusual about a mom wanting her daughter's room to be neat. After all, mom works hard to keep the house in order and she shouldn't have to keep her daughter's bedroom door closed to avoid the frustration of seeing the clutter every time she walks past. And there's nothing strange about a dad wanting his son to keep an extra car length between his car and the one in front of him when he's driving. After all, that's how dad drives. And aren't parents supposed to show their children how to do things right?

94 Absolutely.

But problems arise when parents confuse what is right with what they prefer.

The parent trap is not simply wanting to have things your way; it's not knowing when your way is *one of many* good ways and when it is the *only* right way.

One of the most common problems I hear from parents at odds with their kids involves this one issue. Parents are trying to get things done their way while the child wants to do things his or her way.

As children get older and life gets more complex, this clash of wills becomes a trap that too many parents and children find difficult to escape.

Parents want their children to do things the same way they do.

The only way I know to escape this trap without causing serious damage is to . . .

95

Understand and appreciate the differences between you and your child.

Easy for me to say, right? But how does a parent go about doing such a thing?

Understanding the differences between you and your child

Here's the trick: To spring the trap and release your child you need to understand and accept the many ways you and your child are different from each other. To help you do this, consider how each of you does things in the following four areas:

✔ STRENGTHS

✔ REWARD NEEDS

✔ SENSE OF TIME

✔ PEOPLE ABILITIES

Let's look at how different you can be.

STRENGTHS

DON is frustrated because his son, David, doesn't have a "killer attitude" when it comes to sports. "He's a loser," Don moans. "I'm making him go out for football this fall so he'll learn how to win. How's he ever going to be successful in life if he doesn't care whether he wins or loses?"

Don and David are alike in that they both love sports and are gifted athletically. But . . .

This is what Don doesn't see . . .

David, like his mother, is very detail-oriented. To understand David, Don needs to realize that his son doesn't pay attention to winning because he focuses on perfecting and delivering excellence. The boy is more interested in improving his own performance than in overcoming an opponent in a challenge that requires only physical strength. The father is wrong about the recipe for success in life. David's passion for excellence and perfection is just as valid for measuring success as his father's passion for winning. Sports that require more finesse—like golf, archery, tennis, or even bowling—will better suit David than the rough and tumble, no pain, no gain sports his father loves. Yet only when Don sees his son as being different from himself will he be able to guide his son instead of butting heads with him.

JENNIFER has just about had it with her son, Jason. She has asked him to do one simple task—take out the garbage once a week—but Jason makes it into a major ordeal every Tuesday morning. One week he puts it on his wagon and takes it out. The next week he spends half an hour strapping it to his skateboard and then has to pick it up three times when it falls off before he gets it to the curb. The next week he gets up at 5:30 A.M. and waits at the end of the driveway to hand it personally to the garbage man. "I can't stand it any more!" wails Jennifer. "I just want the garbage taken out the right way. What's going to happen when he's on his own and doesn't have time to waste fooling around?"

This is what Jennifer doesn't see . . .

The issue isn't that Jason refuses to take out the garbage; it's his method of doing it. Jason is taking out the garbage the way he likes to do everything. He enjoys finding new and different ways to do things, a fine creative ability. Jennifer doesn't recognize Jason's creativity, however, because all she sees is inefficiency. To her, taking out the garbage is a simple, dull chore that requires efficiency, not creativity. So while she has settled on the "right" (i.e., most efficient) way of getting the garbage to the curb, Jason is more interested in making the task interesting.

The "fooling around" she thinks she sees is really her son's creativity, which can be a great asset in life if he's encouraged to develop it. We hope Jennifer will step back and release the trap she has set for her son when she realizes that Jason's priorities in completing a task differ from her priorities in assigning it. If she tries to see what's really going on, she will find an emerging adult that needs to be guided rather than nagged. And both she and her son will be happier.

Out of the trap

Do you expect your child to complete tasks a certain way even though they could be done some other way?

Consider the difference between what is truly a matter of "right and wrong" and what "seems right" to you because of your own natural abilities. It is one of the most critical observations parents need to make. Check your natural strengths against your child's in every conflict. Understanding this will help keep you from placing unrealistic expectations on your child.

What was the last conflict you had with your child? Did it involve a matter of right and wrong or personal preference? What can you do to avoid conflicts that are only a matter of personal preference?

REWARD NEEDS

SAM is concerned that his daughter, Sarah, doesn't seem to have much self-confidence. "She doesn't speak up much," he says, "and I don't know why. She's nearly a straight-A student, but she seems sad and lonely much of the time. I worry that she'll be this way as an adult and that it will keep her from getting ahead in life. I tell her I love her but it doesn't seem to make much difference."

This is what Sam doesn't see . . .

Sarah has little idea that she does anything well. Her father's pleasure concerning her good grades is blotted out by his displeasure over her quiet personality. He rarely, if ever, talks to her about school except to ask how her work compares to that of the other children. His own passion to meet requirements is becoming a burden to his daughter. Her seeming lack of "self-confidence" would be replaced by real confidence if Sam could learn to praise Sarah for her good grades, which are more important to her than the approval of her peers.

■ ■ ■ ■ ■ ■ ■ ■ ■ ■ ■ ■

MARILYN grabbed my arm after I finished speaking. Big tears were on the verge of spilling onto her cheeks. "Nobody appreciates what I do," she whispered. "I work thirty hours a week, manage the house, and take care of the kids. But nobody ever says a word about it. It's not that I don't love what I do. It's just that it doesn't seem to make a difference to anybody."

This is what Marilyn doesn't see . . .

What she does makes a great deal of difference in her family nest, and her family knows that. But she lives in a home where everyone still needs to learn the importance of rewarding fellow-nesters for their good work. So she will always feel a lack somewhere in her work until someone gives her the rewards she deserves.

Out of the trap

The parent trap keeps families from rewarding one another for good work. Every home ought to be characterized by enthusiasm for "a job well done" rather than by constant criticism for things left undone or done "the wrong way" because no one gets the chance to work in a way that best suits their gifts and abilities. If you fail to reward your children for things that are important to them, don't expect them to appreciate what is important to you.

What your child needs to hear may be quite different from what you need to hear. If they receive no rewards from you, they will find them elsewhere.

SENSE OF TIME

ANNA is concerned that her son, Alan, won't finish his homework. "He starts it when I insist, but he won't stay

101

focused long enough to get it done. I keep pointing out his assignment list, but he keeps wandering off to take care of other things around the house. He's such a procrastinator that he's going to flunk if he's not careful. What's he going to become with that kind of an attitude? A bum?"

This is what Anna doesn't see . . .

 Alan focuses better when he has to work in a hurry. Ordinary homework doesn't present enough real pressure to make it interesting. It isn't that Alan is going to be a bum; it's that he needs to find a career that will constantly challenge him. And of course he will ultimately need to learn to manage less-than-challenging tasks, which are an inevitable part of every job. Anna needs to figure out some REAL deadlines for Alan, such as insisting that an assignment be completed before eating a snack. Anna's own style of using time deliberately and carefully clashes with her son's need for a high-intensity situation. If the two of them were cooking utensils, she'd be a crockpot and he'd be a pressure cooker. They both serve a purpose, but you'll have a wretched meal if you use one when the other is called for. If Anna can find the right balance, she will be a valuable asset in guiding her son toward a career that matches his personality.

. . . .

RON is growing tired of his daughter's inability to tell a story in a reasonable amount of time. "Her stories are like black holes," Ron says while holding his head. "The further in you get, the bigger they get. She gets so immersed in details that everyone forgets what the story is about before she gets anywhere near the end. We're always interrupting her to say, 'Okay, so what's the point?' Can you imagine her in a business setting?" he adds, rolling his eyes.

This is what Ron doesn't see . . .

His daughter is being careful with her story. She sees so many details that she loses her way trying to get through them. Making her hurry frustrates her because details cause her to lose her sense of time. Her methodical style is part of the way she has been designed.

A wise parent will help her find her way through the details rather than leave her lost in the middle of them. As for her chances of success in the marketplace, employers are happy to have detail-oriented people in many positions.

Out of the trap

We all have built-in chronometers, our own unique sense of time. Consider how you move compared to your teenagers; compare them to each other.

You'll see the difference. A wise parent understands the difference and compensates for it.

Time is a critical component in letting a child go. Describe in writing the two most significant differences between you and your child in the ways you use time.

103

PEOPLE ABILITIES

KAY is starting to worry about her daughter's lack of social skills. "Karen never socializes," Kay moans. "As a child, she never shared her toys and wouldn't color with the other children. Now, as a teenager, she has little interest in being with people. She is totally unlike me or her father. What can I do to change her before she's on her own?"

This is what Kay doesn't see . . .

Karen works best alone. Her toys are her tools. Why should she color with someone else when she has her own work? There are, of course, times to teach Karen to share, but Kay should select them carefully. Working well alone is a good skill to have, and Kay needs to respect her daughter's desire to work alone, understanding it as an innate habit, not a social problem.

. . . .

FRED is upset with his son for the very opposite reason. "Johnny won't do anything by himself. He insists on having people around all the time. He won't do homework unless there are people in the room. He doesn't like to sit by himself and he's always in trouble at school for talking. He's driving everyone nuts. I love to get alone with a good book and read. But I can't get ANYWHERE alone since we've had Johnny."

This is what Fred doesn't see . . .

Johnny does his best work in cooperation with other people. Interaction with others helps him stay focused. He is totally different from his dad in this key people-ability, an ability that should be a tremendous asset as an adult. A smart dad will accommodate his son's abilities whenever he can while he figures out some way to get the quiet time he needs.

Out of the trap

Understand how your child works with people. Does it match up well with yours? Do you both enjoy working alone? Does one of you enjoy working with people while the other likes to influence people? If both of you influence people, you may find yourselves arguing a lot.

How do your people abilities compare with those of your child? In what ways are they different? What conflicts does this cause?

Staying out of the parent trap

Parents who see their child's different approach to a chore as a battle of wills will become fearful parents. And if they fail to make their home big enough for the child's natural way of doing things as well as for their own, their fears may become self-fulfilling prophecies.

105

However, when you understand and accept that your child's way of doing things is as valid as your own, you are in the proper position for letting go. And you will become very comfortable in the "letting go" position as you practice it for the next few crucial years.

David's Story
Handing Him the Keys

DRIVING LESSONS

I didn't think it would bother me as much as it did. All he wanted was . . . my car. He's always used my stuff, worn my clothes. All the kids have. Nothing I own has been off-limits to them. In fact, I like having them use my stuff. It makes me feel connected to them. That's why this feeling surprised me when he asked for the keys the first time. We had just finished dinner when he put his arm on my shoulder and crooned, "Well, Dad, can I have the keys?"

"My k-keys?" I stammered. "Uh, you just got your license. Why are you in such a hurry?" I know my response caught him off guard.

"I just wanted to drive over to Gramma's and take her for a ride."

In my car. My new car.

"The keys are hanging up," I answered, smiling through gritted teeth. I knew then that this driving stuff was about a lot more than my son's skill behind the wheel, or even his freedom. It was not going to be as easy as I had thought.

#15

What do you appreciate the most about your child? What does your child do in a way that is different from the way you would do it but that you think is neat? Write about it in your journal—and tell your kid.

#16

Does your child appreciate what you do differently? Probably not if the only time he or she hears about it is when something is wrong. Point out to your child something you enjoyed doing and take the time to explain how you did it and what you enjoyed most about doing it.

#17

Schedule a lunch with a parent who has a child that seems to be very different from both the mother and the father and yet seems to be thriving. Take along your journal and jot down some of the secrets of their home.

Chapter Six

A Necessary Tension

Giving Up Control without Losing Authority

Art is not about things as they are, but things as they matter.

—LELAND RYKEN

**OME PARENTS HAVE A DETAILED** description of what they want their kids to be like when they are young, but their descriptions often do not grow with the child. They stay focused on do's and don'ts, never shifting to whys and why nots. As a result, these parents wind up with adult children rather than young adults. And they don't have a clue as to why or how it happened.

Before your child gets any older, take time to think about what your expectations really are. What do you want your young adult to be like when he or she is fifteen? sixteen? seventeen? eighteen? Do you want . . .

* *A fifteen-year-old who goes to bed every night at nine o'clock?*

* *A sixteen-year-old who never drinks pop without asking you first?*

* *A seventeen-year-old who doesn't get herself pregnant in high school?*

* *An eighteen-year-old who has never used drugs?*

Or do you want a child who knows how to make wise choices, who knows when to ask questions, who knows how to follow advice, who understands that poor choices have inherent consequences (not just parentally imposed consequences)?

111

If the target below showed your goals in parenting your teenager, what would be in the circles surrounding the bullseye? (For example, good grooming, good grades, neatness, obedience, honesty, healthy self-image, conformity to family values, politeness, regular church attendance, respect for authority, approved friends.) Would your target look like this one? How would it be different?

In your journal or on a separate piece of paper, list in descending order of importance ten things you want your teenager to master before he or she leaves home. On the last line write your primary goal for your teenager's life. As you do so, keep in mind the bullseye of parenting:

To release into the world a healthy, well-adjusted young adult.

Are you willing to do whatever it takes to hit the bullseye?

Yes, I said, *"Whatever it takes!"* That means compromising when your teen has needs that conflict with yours, being patient when your teen disappoints you, and respecting your teen even when you're baffled as to how he or she got to be so different from you.

If you're ready, truly ready, sign up now . . .

If you're like most parents, you arrived on the parent-of-a-teenager scene believing that your child will want to do things

112 you don't like and that you'll be powerless to do much about

Out of the Nest PARENT PACT

I, the parent of

_____,

agree to do whatever it takes to properly launch this young adult into the world.

_____

Signature

it. Here are three things you can do to begin to give up control without losing authority.

1.

Focus

Focus, *n., a state or condition permitting clear perception or understanding.*

REMEMBER the first time you boxed up baby clothes that your child had outgrown? Remember how you sat on the floor, held up each piece, and sighed longingly?

113

Go ahead and sigh now. Sigh long and hard. Sigh until all your sighing is used up.

All sighed out? Ready to admit that what's past is past?

Good. Now you can begin to look at your growing teenager without seeing a helpless, dependent youngster.

Okay, I'm ready to start looking at my child as a young adult . . . (sigh)

If you can do this, you're farther along than one mom I talked to the other day. She was furious that their church youth group was offering a spring break ski trip for junior high kids. Under no conditions would she allow her thirteen-year-old to attend the all-day outing. She even spent hours on the phone raging to other parents about the horror of such an activity for teenagers so young. She ripped her kid out of the group and announced that her family would attend church somewhere else.

This mom is so focused on raising a "child" that she can't see the young adult ready to emerge. And because her focus is wrong, she is missing an opportunity to begin the letting go process in a safe, structured environment.

What will happen? One day she'll be jolted by some unexpected behavior in her daughter and her fuzzy focus will become suddenly clear. But the picture she sees won't be pretty. In fact, she may not even recognize her daughter, and she will have lost the opportunity to be a presence in her teenager's life because she denied the truth that is now before her.

2.

Presence

Presence, *n., the state of being in one place and not elsewhere; of being within sight or call, at hand; the fact of being in company, attendance, or association.*

THERE is a place in your child's life that only parents can fill. But it's easy for moms and dads to get left behind in their child's life due to life's daily pressures. Which ones apply to you?

❏ personal problems

❏ other children

❏ work

❏ _____ (fill in the blank)   **115**

Everything from daycare to TVs that serve as babysitters makes it convenient for parents to *watch* their kids grow up rather than participate in the process.

Parents who have chosen the role of bystander rather than participant throughout their child's life will be seen as intruders if they try at this late date to involve themselves in the letting go process. But you can't let your child go if you have no presence in his or her life.

Of course, some parents create a negative presence, which is of little value when it comes to letting go. What is essential for "good" letting-go is a strong, healthy, positive presence.

Life is complicated. There are times when we have little choice as to the amount of presence we can have in our child's life. And it's easy to feel guilty about it. The truth is, though, we need to be that "presence" in any way we can.

But don't despair if you have neglected this important aspect. There are ways to reclaim or strengthen your presence. Here are four places where you can have a healthy presence in your child's life.

At Activities

Remember when you hung on the refrigerator all the art and school work your kids did? Much of their good work now is done away from home in a tennis match or a band performance or a school debate. Seeing your face in the crowd at those events now is as important as it was then to see their artwork on the fridge.

Too many parents wait until dinnertime to learn about special activities of the day. It is far better to participate in those experiences than to hear about them. Your presence is needed at as many functions as you can manage.

Scheduling can be a nightmare, I know, especially when **116** you have more than one child in addition to a demanding job.

It's the biggest excuse for parental absence at special activities. If you use that excuse frequently, make sure it truly is a scheduling problem and not your lack of interest. (If it is a scheduling problem, there will be times when you can work it out in favor of your child.)

True, band concerts can be boring. And dance recitals may put you to sleep. And it can be miserable standing out in the rain at track meets. But hey, those are your kids. And what they're doing is important. So go.

Then when the day comes that you have something important to say, they may be willing to listen—because they will remember when you went out of your way to listen to (or watch) what was important to them.

Make your presence felt.

Are there grandparents or family friends who could partner with you to make their presence felt. Teenagers often grow significantly in relationships with caring adults other than their parents.

At Bedtime

If it is important to talk with children when they are young, it's even more important as they become young adults. It gets tougher as they get older to make nightly trips to the bedroom as their bedtime gets later and later. But your quiet

presence on the edge of the bed at the end of a busy day is crucial, a moment of quality time that cannot be replaced.

In Fun

Doug began taking his fifteen-year-old daughter to one movie a month. He had no agenda except to have fun with her. He let her choose the movie, and he bought each of them a large popcorn and soft drink.

After several months, Doug was amazed at the huge door of communication that had opened between him and his daughter.

Many parents get so busy with work, homes, hobbies, and the obligations of raising children that they fail to include fun times as part of the process.

Few relationships will grow and develop if shared leisure time is not part of them. Your presence and involvement in fun times sets the stage for letting your child go—and go well.

In Work

Just as there is a time for fun with your child, there is a time for work as well. And sharing both with your offspring can do wonders.

The opportunity to involve yourself in the work of your child is too important to miss because working together fosters growth and connection in subtle yet deep ways.

Many parents realize the value of work in a child's development, but few realize the need for parental involvement. Unfortunately, many parents see their role as that of giving work assignments and then grading the performance. That's a presence, all right, but not the kind you want.

Children are not servants who are to be assigned chores that adults don't want to do. They need to think of work as much more than the performance of unwanted chores; they need to learn that it is deeply rewarding.

Find work in which your child can operate as your equal and feel your enthusiasm. The shared experience as well as the

119

dialogue that takes place is critical to strengthening the strands of your changing relationship.

3.

Control

Control, *n., power or authority to guide or manage*

YOU can't begin to give a young adult control of his or her life if you don't have it to give. And you can't let your child go if he or she is already gone.

Evaluate yourself in the following areas to see if you need to "get control" before you can let go:

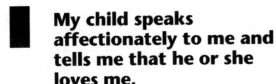

My child speaks affectionately to me and tells me that he or she loves me.

❒ YES   ❒ NO

Verbal and physical communication of affection for one another is crucial to your relationship. Daily hugs and "I love yous" are essential to the letting-go process. If they are missing, you must get them back.

This may sound impossible after years of neglect. But it can be turned around if you're willing to make the effort.

One mom started writing daily notes to her teenage daughter and putting them in her schoolbooks every evening. A dad started giving big hugs to his son (who was already larger than he was) every day. He worried that he'd waited too long, that the son was too big, too old, and wouldn't allow it. He also admitted how odd it felt because they hadn't hugged for years. At first the son acted as if he didn't like it much, but the father kept it up. Soon the father could feel his son soften while he was hugging him, and after a while the son began hugging back.

All of us, parent or almost-adult, need outward displays of love and affection from the important people in our lives. Teenagers who don't get such affection often search for it elsewhere.

If that gulf lies between you and your child, you can't expect to have any control beyond the kind that is harsh and argumentative, and that is very little control at all.

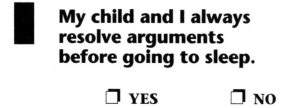

My child and I always resolve arguments before going to sleep.

❐ YES   ❐ NO

Inevitably you and your growing child will get into some dandy arguments. You will yell and shout and say things that shouldn't be said. Neither of you will change your opinion and both of you will leave the argument angry and upset. But let me warn you. If you don't take control of resolving these arguments, they will destroy your ability to let go of your child properly. Don't transfer the control of this important area to your child by waiting for him or her to come to you.

Promise yourself that you will never allow your child to go to bed angry. I don't care if it means staying up all night until you talk through it. I don't care if it means calling in late for work and keeping your child home from school until it is resolved. You don't always have to agree with your child, and vice versa, but you do have to control how you work through disagreements.

121

If you don't, you will be in no position to let your child go; your child will already be gone.

 ## My child does things when I ask.

☐ **YES**   ☐ **NO**

You have to control the spirit of cooperation in your relationship with your child. I am not speaking about chores or assignments. Because of your developing relationship, your young adult child is going to have to learn how to cooperate with you without making it law. Legislation around your home should be turning into suggestions and advice. Your child needs to practice *choosing* to pay attention to what you prefer. Otherwise, that infamous teenaged "deaf-ear" will drive you to the edge of insanity.

How is this spirit of cooperation fostered by what you say and how you say it? It has everything to do with the difference between a request and a command. For example . . .

> "Jackson, will you help me shovel the driveway? I'm running late and I'm really tired."

> "Janet, will you go out to the garage and get a piecrust from the freezer? I have my hands in the cherries, and I want to get the pie in the oven before the company comes."

> "Bill, can you be home by 5:30? That's when dinner will be ready."

Many parents withdraw from involving their children in dialogue because they don't like the whining that often accompanies the request. They'd rather perform the task themselves than put up with the "bellyaching." But a little extra work to push through the complaining, and a little more effort at explaining why the job needs to be done will pay off. And most important, it will set the stage for letting your child go on time.

 My child will sit down and talk with me when I ask.

☐ YES   ☐ NO

The exchange of words between you and your child becomes more important the older your child gets. The most common complaint I get from parents is that their teenagers don't talk to them anymore.

To let your child go successfully, you must assume responsibility for the dialogue between the two of you.

I heard one parent grumble, "I want to talk more to my teenager, but there is so much good television to watch at night."

We all know there isn't *that* much good on television. And certainly nothing that's more important than communication with our kids. Yes, it takes time to talk; it takes effort to build rapport; it takes courage to make ourselves vulnerable to our kids; and if television (or anything else) is that important to us, it may even take sacrifice.

But consider the options: would you rather miss an episode of your favorite sit-com or news magazine or miss finding **123**

out that your daughter is being pressured by her boyfriend to have sex?

If you're serious about truly communicating with your teen, it may mean buying chips and soda and finding something to enjoy about your son's favorite program. It may mean learning to understand music that sounds like noise to you. It may mean making your child's favorite tea and sitting up late at night and talking about anything and everything.

Whatever it means, it's imperative to do it. Failing to nurture conversation with your offspring as early as possible will cause suspicion if you try to do it later on. Show real interest, beginning now, without threatening to invade their privacy, and they'll respond, especially if you make it a habit. If the habit of communication is not established early and maintained during these in-between years, you will not be able to effectively let your child go. Once children are convinced that their parents are not truly interested in what they think and feel, they lose interest in what the parents think and feel.

Finding the Bullseye

Go back to the target at the beginning of this chapter. Do you want to revise it in any way? Are you aiming at what you want to hit or are you firing arrows at peripheral issues? Are you getting the practice you need to hit a bullseye?

As soon as you've got your target set properly, we'll find out how to hit that bullseye.

DRIVING LESSONS

David's Story
Crash

Everything had gone perfectly. David had finished driving school and become the safest driver in the family. He ran errands for me, chauffeured his brothers and sisters, and took himself to the orthodontist. We were stunned, therefore, when the phone rang one afternoon and I heard an alien-like voice telling me the news that causes every parent's heart to stop: "Your son has been in an accident." My husband and I rushed to the scene and found our son being treated by paramedics for minor injuries. Shivering in the middle of that snow-covered intersection, I looked around at the parts of our new car strewn everywhere. Even though it was a total loss, I felt indescribable relief.

And that's what we tried to express to our son later that night as the three of us had a long talk around the kitchen table. We had never had such a serious conversation with him, and our questions yanked him out of his childhood. What happened? Whose fault was it? Who is going to pay what the insurance doesn't cover?

We worked through the questions until we got answers everyone could live with, but there is more ahead. He will have to attend his court date. He will have to get a part-time job to pay for the damage. And all of us will have to learn how to recover when a child has an adult-sized accident.

Getting STARTED

#18   Have you hugged your kid today? The phrase has become almost a joke, but the idea is right on. And, more important, has your kid hugged you? A relationship must be two-sided if it is to grow and deepen.

#19   Maybe you think your child has outgrown bedtime stories. Not so. Just change "story" to "conversation." Schedule a bedtime conversation with your teenager on a regular basis. But lay some ground rules for yourself first. For example, no arguing, no punishing, no making a point. This is just a time for two human beings to reflect on life and some of the crazy things each of you faces in the different worlds you live in.

#20   What area of control/input do you have to take back that you gave up prematurely. Think very carefully about this and write about it in your journal. How are you going to accomplish it?

Chapter Seven

Finding Your Voice

Taking Your Rightful Place
in Your Child's Life

Our life is
frittered away
by detail . . .
simplify, simplify.

—HENRY DAVID THOREAU

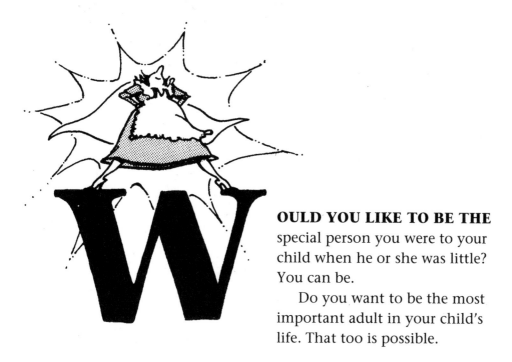

WOULD YOU LIKE TO BE THE special person you were to your child when he or she was little? You can be.

Do you want to be the most important adult in your child's life. That too is possible.

The Moment of Perception

As your relationship with your child continues to stretch and grow into something brand new, one thing remains the same. It is something that you probably take so much for granted that you don't even think about how powerful it is. You used it the first time you held your baby close and whispered into his or her ear. You used it to soothe your little girl when she was frightened and to calm your little boy when he couldn't sleep. It is your lifeline to your child's soul.

It is your voice.

Unfortunately, about the time your son's voice changes, so does yours. But not for the better. While his moves down an octave due to maturity, yours goes up several pitches due to fear. Fear that you are losing control. Fear that your son has more courage than common sense. Fear that your daughter is too nice to "just say no."

This fear begins its crescendo when children reach puberty because that is when parents suddenly realize the potentially **131** serious consequences of the decisions their offspring are making.

This is tragic because your voice still has the power to be used for good in your child's life, but desperation may cause you to unintentionally use it in a harmful way.

Which of the following sounds is most like your voice as it echoes through your home?

- **a jack-hammer (controling)**
- **waves lapping on the shore (soothing)**
- **a gavel (judging)**
- **a gentle breeze (refreshing)**

If your voice sounds like a jack-hammer or a gavel (or something worse) your children are hearing fear, not love;

they're hearing doubt, not faith. And what the tone of your voice communicates about your children is what they will believe about themselves.

You can use your voice like a whip to try to maintain control over your children, or you can use it like a wand to wave over them in blessing. If you do the latter, you will never be far away from your children—even as they enter the frightening world of early adulthood.

Your voice is a sound that no one can reproduce, and it makes five distinctive tones that every child needs to hear.

1.

Your Welcoming Voice

It tells your child that everything is all right.

YOU were the first one to greet your child, mom. The doctor laid the baby on your chest, and you squeezed him and whispered how happy you were to finally meet him. You wrapped yourself around him with soft words and whispered over and over how much you loved him, how you would always protect him, and how everything would be all right.

Your voice was the first thing your children recognized about you. After being apart for even a short time, your voice welcomed them as if they had been away for years. Your voice always said, "You are welcome here beside me because you are my child. Nothing you can do will ever make you unwelcome." **133**

How do you talk to your young adult? Do your words still soothe and welcome?

The world is a tough place to adjust to. It's easy for parents to forget how important daily words of welcome are to children.

Think about your voice patterns. Are you giving your child a warm welcome into the adult world?

How does your welcoming voice sound?

Is it *warm?*

    ☐ YES   ☐ NO

Is it *unhurried?*

    ☐ YES   ☐ NO

Is it *focused?*

    ☐ YES   ☐ NO

Is it *sincere?*

    ☐ YES   ☐ NO

Is it *accepting?*

    ☐ YES   ☐ NO

If you have ever been in the parking lot of a junior high school when school lets out, you know what bedlam is. When I go to pick up Talia I park in the middle of the commotion, get out of the car, stand on the bumper, and hold up a huge sign that says in bright, bold purple letters . . .

I get a kick when she comes out of the building, looks around, and sees her name screaming from above the crowd as all the kids point at me. And her reaction is always the same. She rolls her eyes, walks to the car, gives me a hug, and says, loudly enough for her friends to hear, "I hate it when you do that, Dad!" But then she settles into the front seat with a sweet little half-smile on her face.

I have welcomed her home.

How to use your welcoming voice

Greet your child every morning with a hug and a kiss and words of welcome. For example, "I'm so glad to have another day to enjoy your company" or "I'm looking forward to the fun time we'll have at the mall tonight."

If you're home when your child gets home, greet him at the door and tell him how glad you are

135

that he is home. Every now and then meet your child at the bus stop and walk the rest of the way home together.

✎ ***If you are away at work when your child arrives at home, call shortly after he or she is due to be home and find out how the day went.*** To be welcomed by someone who loves you is an important moment for children, especially young teens. Your voice should be the one constant, accepting sound they hear. If they do, they will always come back to hear more.

2.

Your Cautioning Voice

It points out hidden dangers to your child.

PARENTS play two important roles in the lives of their children. They are both a rear-view mirror and a pair of binoculars. They see things from the past that might creep up and cause harm, and they see dangers off in the darkness.

When your child was young and got so engrossed in playing baseball that she ran into the street without looking for cars, you learned the importance of using your voice to caution her of danger. Your child became so familiar with your voice that he or she could sense the degree of urgency in it and knew when it was necessary to heed your warnings almost without thinking. And you learned how important it was to use your most urgent-sounding voice only when true danger was imminent. Otherwise your child would become deaf to your warnings.

We hope your child is to the point that you no longer have to issue warnings to get out of the street, but some of the warnings you have to give are just as important. And you still need to be careful not to use your voice in a way that gives the same sense of urgency to everything.

How does your cautioning voice sound?

Is it *urgent?*

❒ **YES** ❒ **NO**

Is it *calm?*

❒ **YES** ❒ **NO**

Is it *direct* and *authoritative?*

❒ **YES** ❒ **NO**

Is it *gentle* but *firm?*

❒ **YES** ❒ **NO**

Perhaps the hardest thing to learn about your cautioning voice is when to use it. The other evening Josh was telling us what he thought about the way a musical piece was being assembled for a school choir presentation. Josh's passion for excellence was coming through loud and clear, but he was sounding a lot like a know-it-all teenager.

"Be careful," I cautioned him at the dinner table.

137

"Careful about what?" he mumbled through a mouthful of mashed potatoes.

"Just be careful how you come across," Debbie chimed in. "You don't know everything."

"I don't know everything, but I know this song. And it sounds like garbage," he snapped. Now Josh was angry that we had confronted him.

We spent the next ten minutes accusing each other of all kinds of bizarre things.

Later that night I realized I had made a significant mistake, and I went to Josh's room to apologize for not handling the episode properly.

"Sometimes it's tough," I said. "You are going to be right a lot of times, but I'm just concerned that you know how to handle being right. People hate a kid who thinks he knows everything. Even if he does."

Josh looked up at me. "I'll be careful, Dad. But I am right, you know."

"Maybe you are. But just remember that there are times when being respectful is more important than being right."

Knowing when and how to use my cautioning voice is a tricky thing.

How to use your cautioning voice

Your cautioning voice has the most potential to wound your child. It uses the sharpest words and generally carries the most energy. To use it effectively . . .

✏ ***Speak gently, remembering that how you say something is as important as what you say.*** Listen to yourself as you speak to your child. Would *you* want to listen to you? Would you want to be spoken to in that way?

138 ✏ *Touch your child affectionately on the arm or*

shoulder when you speak. Don't sit so far away. Make yourself touchable.

✐ ***Calm down and regain your composure before speaking.*** Do NOT force a conversation when you are angry. A few minutes' break will help, not hurt, the situation.

✐ ***Be direct and to the point.*** Make sure your voice carries the authority the situation calls for. Being *too* nice can be just as damaging as being too angry.

All the healthy adults I know have someone in their lives who regularly points out their blind spots. Children need this too, but they need to have it done in a special way: with understanding and compassion. Children are tender; they need to be bent not broken.

Parents can do this better than anyone else for two simple reasons: they know their children the best, and they love them the most.

3.
Your
Correcting
Voice

*It divides truth from lie
for your child.*

EVERY child needs someone who serves as a source of reason and truth. You've always been that person, as well you should be. When your child was younger, you could serve up generous portions of truth and mix in a lot of your personal beliefs and preferences. In fact, for a long time you got away with that final, ultimate parental answer to prolonged questioning: ***"Because I said so, that's why."*** Your little ones accepted your interpretation of the world. Their tiny ears strained to hear the directions that you were willing and eager to give.

Although they are bigger now, they need every bit as much wisdom to distinguish truth from lies. But they're not so naive any more. Now when you mix personal preferences with truth they smell it a mile away and won't have anything to do with it. The danger of this is that they may reject truth when all they are really trying to avoid is your preference.

Your voice of truth is the most sobering of your five voices. It is uncompromising and wise—but only when it is not diluted by your biases.

The purpose for your voice of correction is not to condemn your child; it is to call your child to a place of safety.

If you remember this one rule concerning your voice of correction you will seldom misuse it:

Don't use your voice to say something is true when it is only your opinion.

How does your correcting voice sound?

Is it *harsh* and *judgmental?*

☐ **YES**   ☐ **NO**

Is it *eager to prove your child wrong?*

☐ **YES**   ☐ **NO**

Does it *gloat?*

☐ **YES**   ☐ **NO**

Is it *angry?*

☐ **YES**   ☐ **NO**

Does it seek to *enforce* rather than to teach?

☐ **YES**   ☐ **NO**

Elaine complained that her daughter never listened to her. "She talks back something fierce," Elaine said, "but what is so odd is that she is just the sweetest girl all the rest of the time. We just can't seem to find the right punishment."

"Have you sat down with her when she wasn't talking back and discussed it with her?" I asked.

"You mean to talk about the kind of punishment she'll get?" Elaine asked.

"No," I replied. "I mean to talk through the whole thing—how she's acting when she loses control, how she should be acting, what she can do to remember how she should act, and what you can do to help her keep control."

"No, I hadn't thought of that."

141

Truth versus opinion

Harry's dad believed that his way was always right, and he made it clear what he thought Harry should do in every circumstance. One day Harry and some friends made counterfeit parking passes to use at school. They were caught and got suspended from classes for a day. Harry admitted that he should have listened to his dad, who had warned him that it was wrong. "But my dad thinks he's right about everything," Harry said. "Nobody in my family listens to him anymore. Not even my mom."

If you use a voice like a siren every time something gets you riled up, you will be like the test of the emergency broadcasting system that is aired every so often as a public service. The siren sound has become so familiar that everyone ignores it.

Most children look for a voice of truth. Sadly, they often have trouble finding it. When parents constantly mix opinion with truth, they make it difficult for their children to discern what is really true. Don't let that happen to your children.

4.
Your Restoring Voice

It offers forgiveness and hope to your child.

GROWING up is difficult, and not just from infancy to adulthood. I mean from the cradle to the grave. Growing up is a lifelong journey filled with potholes and detours and bumps and bruises. How many mistakes do you think each one of us will make before we die? How many bad choices? How many stupid choices? We may learn, but it's usually the hard way. Our children are no different.

Of course they'll do stupid things, just as we do. And they'll do the same stupid things over and over, even when we warn them, even when they know better. So your child will spend a lifetime listening for a voice that offers forgiveness and hope. Life is tough enough without a burden of guilt weighing them down. They need to hear words of forgiveness. Often.

While writing this book, I held a number of luncheons for moms to find out their thoughts about some of these ideas. I was surprised to find out how many moms were harboring anger against their children.

"We go through this clothes thing every morning," one mom told me. "Every morning I know we're going to fight about what she's going to wear to school. It makes me angry just thinking about it."

It doesn't take a throat specialist to know that this mom's voice of forgiveness is a little hoarse. Especially in the mornings.

The voice of forgiveness remembers the ultimate goal. Do you?

The goal of parenting is to deliver a healthy young adult into the world.

How Does Your Restoring Voice Sound?

Does it hold a *grudge?*

❐ **YES** ❐ **NO** **143**

Does it *seek retribution?*

☐ **YES**   ☐ **NO**

Does it *remind of past failures?*

☐ **YES**   ☐ **NO**

Is it *easily irritated?*

☐ **YES**   ☐ **NO**

Does it *condemn* rather than release?

☐ **YES**   ☐ **NO**

How to use your restoring voice

Nothing is as painful to a young adult as the unforgiving voice of a parent. On the other hand, the voice of a parent who restores a child through forgiveness to hope is a beautiful sound, and no one in a child's life is in a better position to release him or her from past failures as a parent. Every time you use your restoring voice you give your child a new start.

Here's how to do it:

✏ ***Keep short accounts.*** Don't keep bringing up past failures and transgressions.

✏ ***Make a point of saying the exact words—"I forgive you"—after a child admits that he or she did something wrong.*** Don't assume that a child knows that he or she is forgiven without being told.

144 ✏ ***Express confidence in your child's ability to get***

things right. How many times has your child been wrong? Does he or she feel as if you have given up hope?

➯ ***Give your child the opportunity to get it right.*** Find ways to allow him or her to earn your trust and confidence.

5.

Your Refreshing Voice

It encourages and re-energizes your child.

"H OW can good water and bad water come from the same fountain," asked a voice long ago.

The answer is, it can't.

In the chaos of all the arguing and yelling in today's homes, children strain to hear words of encouragement. The sweet sound of a voice that refreshes is so satisfying that children of all ages find it irresistible.

Many parents find this voice difficult to master because they haven't encouraged anyone for a long time, let alone their children. They have sunk so deeply into themselves that anyone who is different or does things differently is an irritation to them.

If that describes you, it's time to practice your refreshing voice.

145

How does your refreshing voice sound?

Is it *intimate?*

☐ **YES**   ☐ **NO**

Is it *occasional?*

☐ **YES**   ☐ **NO**

Is it *connecting?*

☐ **YES**   ☐ **NO**

Is it *encouraging?*

☐ **YES**   ☐ **NO**

Is it *non-existent?*

☐ **YES**   ☐ **NO**

How to use your refreshing voice

A word of encouragement is the the most refreshing sound your emerging adult can hear—even more refreshing than words of welcome and forgiveness. Encouragement fills your child with energy and vitality, with purpose and meaning. It is a sound children yearn to hear for their entire lives.

Only a few lessons are necessary to recover your voice of **146** refreshment.

Associate your child's name with his or her positive qualities.

Remember how much care you took to find the right name for your child? You looked for that special configuration of letters that represented who your child was. Remember saying things like "He doesn't look like a Fred!" or "She doesn't look like a Camille!"?

And you were right. When you finally chose a name, it represented all the passions you would soon discover in your child. So now when you say the name, memories flood your mind of things your daughter does, of passions that are uniquely your son's.

The names and nicknames you give your child, and the way you say them, are among the most powerful sounds your voice makes.

Listen to the sounds of encouragement in the way you say these names:

ALLISA, how marvelously you drew that sketch!

STEVE, nice job waxing the car!

TIMOTHY, beautiful job painting those corners!

SARAH, you work so well alone.

MARIE, your kindness made that woman smile.

Connecting your children's name to their passion encourages **147** them in a unique way. It connects them to the things that give them energy and that make them feel good about themselves. Think of your child's name as a combination of words that reveals what a unique and marvelous creature he or she is becoming. When you do this, you won't have any trouble using the right voice when you say it.

Refresh your child face to face, eye to eye.

Young adults are moving targets. The encouragement they need to launch them into healthy adulthood is like a well-balanced meal—desirable, but who has time? You will be tempted to shout at the back of her head as she races through the house and to talk to the side of his face while he watches television.

Don't settle for that.

Smack dab in the center of your young adult's face are two glassy, glowing orbs called eyes. Your child sees the world through these tiny windows, and when you look into them, you can see your child.

When moms and dads place themselves face-to-face with their children, unusual things happen. They choose their words more carefully; they control their emotions; communication begins to flower.

MaryBeth has a fourteen-year-old daughter. After talking to me about this, she went home and asked her daughter to sit down next to her. They made small talk for a few moments, and then MaryBeth stopped and said, "Just sit there for a minute. I want to look at your eyes and see if they are as gorgeous as they always were."

The daughter shifted uncomfortably as her mother looked into her eyes. "Why are you doing this?" she asked, her eyes darting around the room. "This is dumb."

148   MaryBeth continued to look into her daughter's eyes as if she was searching for someone. Then, after a few more seconds, tears started to flow from her daughter's eyes.

"Oh, sweetheart, what's wrong," the mother said, reaching out and pulling her daughter into her arms. "I didn't mean to upset you."

Sobbing in her mother's arms, the girl whispered in a muffled voice, "You never look at me like that anymore."

MaryBeth started to cry as she related the story to me.

"I will never forget that," she said softly.

Finding your child's eyes when you speak is like finding a vein when you give an injection. It's the most direct way of administering a prescription for health.

If eyes are the "windows of the soul," that's where we should direct words of encouragement, because they are meant for the soul, not for the kitchen floor.

Before children know a single word, parents communicate with them through their eyes. Remember what it was like to look for your child behind those big, brown eyes, knowing there was a person in there waiting to come out, wondering what he or she would be like?

When was the last time you looked into your child's eyes? Are they still brown? Are they still big? Can you still communicate with your eyes? Do you know how to say "I love you" to your child by the way you look at him or her?

149

Encourage from a proper distance.

As children grow up they inevitably move farther away. At first it's just a few inches—like when they learn to crawl. Then it's to the backyard to play. Then it's to the friend's house across the street. And then . . . before you know it you're talking to your son at camp in another state. Or you're reading a letter from your daughter written during a school trip to the other side of the world.

Your voice needs to adjust to all of those distances because the need to be refreshed and encouraged doesn't diminish as the distance between you increases.

You can create clever ways to manage the distances between you and your child so that your voice can be heard in all types of situations, no matter the distance. By doing so you will never feel disconnected. You will always be near.

 ### Protect your voice from overuse or misuse.

Your voice may be the most powerful tool you have as a parent, so think before you use it. Think hard. Are you using it to build up or tear down?

This stage in your child's life is measured by degrees of help or harm. As long as your mouth is closed, you can't misuse your voice. But the moment you open it you are in danger of using it the wrong way.

So ask yourself this question:

When I open my mouth am I . . .

Welcoming?

Cautioning?

Correcting?

Forgiving?

150   *Encouraging?*

If the answer to any of these is no, think about how you can improve. Figure out what you can do to strengthen your voice so that it can be heard loudly and clearly when you need to use it. And practice making it beautiful so that your children want to listen when you have something to say.

Sara's Story
Keeping My Mouth Shut

DRIVING LESSONS

When you have been driving as long as I have, you forget how many decisions you make in a simple, five-minute trip to the grocery store. I can't imagine my daughter making all the right ones. She pulls into crowded traffic, stops too quickly, doesn't signal properly, and changes lanes too suddenly.

So the problem for me is how to sit beside her and not scream. I see all of the things she is doing wrong. Somehow we manage to make it through these trips safely, but I don't know how. I want to yell and point at all of the things she's not seeing, but I know that's not the right way to help her. I've tried closing my eyes, but that's just plain dangerous. So I sit there, my eyes bulging in terror, making choking noises when I see us running up the rear end of a semi, praying that she will see it soon enough. It's hard for me to keep my mouth shut and let her learn the hard way, like I did. The funny thing is, I don't remember my mom or dad ever riding with me during my first driving days, and I turned out fine. I suppose my daughter will too.

#21

You have to commit to making your voice heard in the bedlam of your child's world. Identify five specific times and places you will talk with your child in the next thirty days.

#22

What one word would you want your child to use to describe your voice to his or her child (your grandchild) in twenty years. Write about this word in your journal.

#23

How does your child's voice sound to you? Mean? Harsh? Kind? Loud? How do you want it to sound? Have a talk with your child about how the voices in your home sound to one another.

My Kid Wants to Be a Sidewalk Musician

**Helping Children
Find Their Lifework**

Personally, I would have sooner written Alice in Wonderland than the whole Encyclopedia Britannica.

—STEPHEN LEACOCK

PART OF THE PROCESS OF LETTING GO is handing over the keys. No, not the car keys. The keys all parents must give to their children is a set that will unlock a box labeled "lifework."

What do you want to be when you grow up?

Kids hear this question so many times it's almost a joke.

"Anything you want to be is fine," we assure them. "If your mind can conceive it and your heart can believe it, you can achieve it."

We give them pep talks to bolster their self-confidence and use positive reinforcement to convince them that they are indeed smart enough to do anything they want to do. But what we *don't* do is help them discover what it is they really *want* to do.

The question of lifework

Kids growing up try on all kinds of futures. They dream about being . . .

a fireman
when their favorite toy is a big red firetruck.

a teacher
when they have their first crush on the new, attractive teacher.

a clown
after attending their first circus.

157

During those early years we listen with interest and affirm their choices with assuring comments, being careful not to deflate their self-esteem or stifle their creativity.

Yet we can't help but wonder what the future really holds.

And we can't help but have a preference about what it should be.

Or can we?

When kids reach their pre-teen years they begin trying on some unusual, even bizarre, futures. But now they're no longer cute or funny; they're alarming.

I've done a lot o' thinking about this, Ma, and I've decided to be a sidewalk musician.

Suddenly our responses to their career goals are not so affirming; they may even be accusing:

What? Are you crazy?
You can't make any money doing that!
Don't expect me to support you for the rest of your life!

At best we shudder and bite our tongues to keep silent.

What went wrong? We only want what's best for our children. Something safe, secure, without problems or risks. So we pray that reality will hit our adult-to-be before the decision-to-be has to be made. But you know what? Reality isn't what we really want because reality stinks. Reality is full of risks and problems, and it is far removed from safety and security.

REALITY CHECK

Go ahead. Ask around. Studies have proven that most employees in the United States hate what they do for a living. They are bored by 9 A.M. Monday morning, live for Friday afternoons, and wish they were doing something else. By mid-life they have changed careers several times and wonder about the very value of their existence.

So . . .

What happened to being a fireman?

A mom called me last week in a panic. Her daughter is graduating from a prestigious northeastern college that costs $24,000 a year to attend, and the daughter knows only one thing about what she wants to do with her life:

159

She wants to do NOTHING related to her degree in psychology.

So now, four years and $100,000 later, the mom is stunned to find out that her daughter still does not know what she wants to be when she grows up.

How do such things happen? Or, a better question, How can we keep such things from happening?

Few things parents do have longer-lasting effects than that of directing their children toward their lifework.

This guidance is crucial. The advice kids hear on the streets and even from many career counselors could mess them up for the rest of their lives.

And whether you know it or not, you hold the keys that will open the best career choices for your child.

Begin early to start thinking about your child's lifework.

RATHER than wait for that magical moment when children mysteriously "know" what to do with the rest of their

160

lives, start talking seriously about it when your children are young and keep right on talking all the way through adolescence. Here are some ways to do this.

 Point out work all around you and talk about it.

As early as possible, explore the work people do and the passions they have for doing it well. Whenever you see people who are enjoying their work, take time to question them about it. Ask what they enjoy most about it, and let your children listen in. Children will begin to notice that some types of work have more appeal to them than other types.

If you pay attention, you could have opportunities every day for your child to hear about the work people do.

For example . . .

161

- ◆✦ **An enthusiastic salesclerk** who enjoys helping people figure out what they need or want.
- ◆✦ **A good teacher** who enjoys helping students learn.
- ◆✦ **An energetic insurance agent** who enjoys selling more policies than anyone else.
- ◆✦ **A successful architect** who enjoys building something exactly right.
- ◆✦ **A contented nurse** who enjoys taking care of people.

People like to talk about what they enjoy, so all of these people, if you ask them, will tell you what makes their work enjoyable.

One day my daughter Megan and I were standing in front of the meat counter at the grocery store watching the girl behind the glass take orders. She had a remarkable amount of energy as she sliced the meat and threw it on the scale. When it was our turn, I asked her if she liked her job.

"Love it," she said.

"What do enjoy most about it?" I asked.

"Easy," she said as she slapped a hunk of turkey onto the scale. "I enjoy trying to slice the exact weight the customer wants on the first try. I've been dead on three times today."

I nodded and gave Megan a knowing glance. She nodded back.

Seize every opportunity to analyze with your child work situations you see, imagining what abilities or passions the person has who is doing the work well.

 Speak openly to other people about the things your child does well and is passionate about.

Fulfillment can be defined only in the language of passion,

and learning the language of passion, like any other language, requires practice in speaking it and hearing it. For children to recognize the opportunities that best match their natural passions, they need to develop the ability to think in terms of what they enjoy doing. Never miss an opportunity to have your child describe to another person what it is that he or she likes about an activity.

The same is true of your own passions and abilities. Speak of them often to your children.

How did you choose your career? Was it a conscious choice or did you take what fell in your lap? Are you happy with your work or do you wish you were doing something else?

Don't settle for a job.

PERHAPS nothing in this discussion is more important than making a distinction between a job and work. I like using the following definitions:

163

job, *n., getting paid to do the things that someone else wants to have done.*

work, *n., getting paid to do the things that you have energy, enthusiasm, and passion for doing.*

Most young adults mimic adults and pursue jobs, doing for someone else what that person wants to have done. Instead, encourage your soon-to-be-adult to pursue *work*, something he or she is enthusiastic about doing.

The difference is like night and day.

Your child's work and the passion that drives it will be different from that of every other person.

With over 300,000 career opportunities, and new ones emerging every day, the problem will never be having too few to choose from. Just remember that ruling something out is as significant as deciding something could be fun. If you throw away 299,000 possible career choices, more than 1,000 are still left.

So why settle for a job?

Find work that uses your child's natural abilities.

Summer employment is one of the best learning laboratories children can have. Rather than let your child take whatever job comes along, help your child think through what he or she would enjoy. Lots can be learned about your child's passions and possible career options by doing this one very simple thing.

As summer job opportunities arise, have your child answer the following questions about each one, then talk about the answers:

❑ **Will I work alone or with other people?**

❑ **Will I do the same thing over and over or will I face new challenges?**

❑ **Will I be given instructions or be asked to figure out things myself?**

❑ **What is the purpose/end result of the work?**

❑ **What (if anything) about the work will be fun? How much of what is fun will be part of my job description?**

Use the answers as a basis for choosing work that is most likely to give your child an opportunity to use his or her natural abilities and passions.

Lessons can, of course, be learned from having an unpleasant job experience too, so whichever way the experience ends up, it will be a great opportunity for your child to learn to evaluate work choices.

Many career counselors and well-meaning friends do not understand the difference between a job and work. Guard against advice that is intended to move your child toward a

165

lifetime of jobs. Anybody can get a job. You want something better for your child. Your child is looking for WORK— something most people know nothing about.

 Find someone who is willing to pay your child for doing work he or she enjoys.

One of our neighbors, a single mom, was expressing her frustration about being unable to find the time to help her seven-year-old with math problems.

"How can she be behind already?" she moaned. "She's only seven."

"Maybe she just needs a little extra help," I volunteered.

"Yeah, right. When am I going to find time to teach math in addition to everything else?"

I stood there a moment remembering a scene I had witnessed in my living room earlier that day. Talia had several of the neighborhood children sitting behind makeshift desks with books and pads of paper. She was busy teaching them whatever kids teach each other at that age.

"Why don't you ask Talia to tutor MaryBeth?" I asked.

"Talia's only nine. How could she do that?"

"Are you kidding? Talia is probably a better teacher at nine than half the teachers in the classroom. She loves to teach. And math is her best subject. She would work with MaryBeth for fun."

Before the afternoon was over, the neighbor had called Talia and offered to pay her five dollars a week to help Mary-Beth with her math problems.

Talia was thrilled, and I was delighted to have her discover that what she enjoyed doing had monetary value.

Money comes.

EVEN though you want your child to know that what he or she enjoys doing has income potential, you want to avoid making money the focus of career searches and evaluations. Never before have young adults had so many career options. With so many options, the possibility of reaching a good one is available to more young people then ever before, especially if they start planning early.

But your child will not be able to take advantage of these opportunities if he or she does not get rid of the idea of looking at career options through the "money window."

When a person is looking for a "job," money is almost always the primary consideration. Why? Because it is *just* a job, and money, not enjoyment or fulfillment, is the only thing you can expect to get from it.

When choosing lifework, money is secondary. So teach your children these concepts about money and work:

Don't choose lifework on the basis of money.

When choosing a career, make money the last consideration. I have counseled many people who are making obscene amounts of money and are miserable because they hate what they are doing. I have also counseled people making less, much less, who love their work and are deliriously happy. There is no direct correlation between the size of a person's salary and their level of happiness.

If you are good at what you do, money will come.

The focus of finding lifework ought to be excellence. There are many places children can use their passion. The better they get at what they are passionate about, the higher the value of their passion. And the more it's valued, the more money they'll probably make.

My experience shows that money follows passion, not vice versa.

Two years ago, Joshua wanted to work at a company that developed video programming and multi-media projects. He wasn't quite fifteen, so he asked the owner if he could work for no pay for the summer so that he could pursue his passion for video production. The owner said sure. Within a month, Josh was taking assignments normally reserved for regular employees. In August, after two and a half months at work, the owner pulled me aside when I was picking up Josh.

"Josh says this is his last week," he said.

"That's right," I said. "Back to school."

The owner shuffled his feet and looked at the ground and then at me.

"I can't afford to lose him. He does good work."

"Thank you," I said. "Make sure you tell him that."

"I don't think you understand," he said. "I mean I can't afford to lose him. I am prepared to offer him a full-time technical position at $30,000 a year, pay for a tutor so that he doesn't have to go back to school, and pay his cab fare to work until he gets his license."

When you are pursuing your passion, the money will come, sometimes slowly, but sometimes more quickly than you're ready for. (After much soul-searching, Joshua turned down the offer because he had a greater passion—to become a high school choral director.)

If you don't enjoy what you do, all the money in the world will not make you happy. But if you love what you do, you are already rich.

Some parents already know this truth. Now we want our children to learn it. If they don't understand their passion and **169** the value of it, they will have a hard time fighting the tide of the "success equals money" culture they are entering.

What's the best way to give your children this key? By introducing them at a young age to work they enjoy and are rewarded for doing.

*Think of college as a place to go
AFTER deciding what lifework
to pursue.*

THE time to experiment with different types of work is *before* college, not during. Work with your child's high school to set up opportunities for your son or daughter (or for his or her entire class) to visit a variety of workplaces. Then generate discussion to help you identify what your child liked and disliked about the different environments. You might think that this is the type of service your tax or tuition dollars are paying for, but it's not. You need to take the initiative.

I do workshops on college campuses with juniors and seniors, and with very little effort we are able to identify several careers that each student would find fulfilling. But there's a problem: Most of them will be graduating in a few months with a totally unrelated degree. They have spent their education dollars preparing for something they have no desire to do. For whatever reasons—practicality, parental desires, or lack of direction—they are finishing degrees they don't like. To see their faces light up when they realize the enjoyable kinds of work their natural abilities offer them is exciting; but to see their faces drop when they realize they have no more time or money to pursue the possibilities is both discouraging and sad.

PHIL was about to graduate with a degree in sociology and an emphasis in youth work. But Phil hated kids. (I'm not making this up.) Phil's passion was weather. He loved everything about weather. He would watch the weather channel the way his friends watched football. His roommates thought he was nuts, and he was dumbfounded when I asked why he wasn't pursuing a career in weather.

"Weather as a career?" he asked.

"Sure," I said. "Why aren't you going into some kind of weather-related career since you love it so much."

"You mean that's all there is to it? You can do something like that just because you like doing it?"

"Well, who do you think is doing the weather?" I asked. "Somebody has to do it. It might as well be you."

Phil got up and walked out of the room. I found him outside under a tree.

"Why didn't anybody tell me I could do that?" he wanted to know. "I would love to go into weather. I would do anything just to be a part of it. I don't want to work with kids. What am I going to do?"

The last I heard Phil had transferred out of school. He then had contacted the manager of a local television station and told him he was interested in working with weather somehow—on the scientific side or on the reporter side—but he didn't really know. The man offered him a summer job, an internship, working around the weather control room so he could watch and evaluate what kind of weather "work" interested him the most and figure out how he could make it into a career.

And he did it in the nick of time.

Is any decision given less thought than the sprint to college after high school graduation? I doubt it. But it's time we asked a few questions about this practice, especially considering the cost and the time involved. Here are a few points to consider and discuss with your college-kid-to-be:

Higher education is a business.

Make no mistake about it. Schools need customers, and your child is a customer. He or she has a checkbook (or is using yours) and the school wants what's in it. School officials will tell you anything you want to hear about the value of their "product" because they want your money. If you think recruitment for higher education is all that different from sales practices at a used car lot, start listening more closely. All the colleges are vying for students. Actively. Without students they will go out of business.

And contrary to what they want you to believe, not everyone needs a traditional college education to qualify for good work choices, especially in today's ever-changing marketplace.

College is a means for reaching goals, not a place for setting them.

Used properly, college is wonderful. But it has to be used at the right time and in the right way. The following are the *wrong* reasons for going to college.

To grow up. College is expensive and it often delays maturity rather than speeds it up. The twenty-year-olds I know who are working are more mature than the twenty-year-olds I know in college. Don't send your kid off to college expecting instant maturity.

To find a career. Send your kid to college after he or she has decided what lifework to pursue. The majority of college graduates get jobs that have nothing to do with their majors. Note the word "jobs" in that sentence. Too often a degree is just a ticket to a job, not a step toward achieving meaningful lifework. What a waste. A waste of time, money, and hopes.

Academic success is not the same as career aptitude.

Somewhere along the line, the question of what children want to do when they grow up is superseded by how well they are doing in school. The thinking seems to be that those who do well in school will naturally have successful careers.

WRONG.

An article about top college students and how well they were doing in their profession said that high-achieving students were no more likely than others to achieve success in their careers. The article concluded that good students were perhaps no more than that—just good students—and that a high grade point average had little to do with career satisfaction or success.

Excellence in studies may be the window to a career, but personal passions are the doorway.

Allow and encourage dreaming.

YOUR children are finding their place in the world, finding a place of fulfilling lifework, maybe the kind that you never had. If you don't enjoy what you do, how do you feel about your child finding enjoyable work? Does it bother you? Believe it or not, some parents want their children to suffer like they did. I hope that's not you.

Here are some things you can say to help your child dream.

Believe that a career you love is within your reach.

Nothing you are passionate about is outside the realm of possibility. Does that mean you can achieve every goal, fulfill every dream, satisfy every desire?

Of course not. There is only one president of the United States, and the odds against achieving that position are high. But I guarantee this—something you are passionate about will open up because it is what you are designed to do.

Don't listen to people who say the career you want is impossible to attain.

Some people may think you are crazy to pursue your passion, but they are usually the ones who are so dulled by their own inability to express passion in their work that they find enthusiasm intimidating. They will try to discourage you. Don't be afraid to prove them wrong.

175

Follow your passion.

Your passions and abilities have been leading in one direction since birth, and you will have the most energy and the most enthusiasm when you are heading that way. So do what you are good at doing; let your natural abilities lead you. But make sure that all your dreams and ambitions are tempered by a heart that desires goodness and a mind that seeks wisdom.

Parents who provide vision and direction without manipulation or guilt will have children who leave the nest with grace and strength, filled with the passion and energy to reach their appointed destination.

And when they do, they will love you through eternity for helping them find it.

Sara's Story
Do As I Say, Not As I Do.

DRIVING LESSONS

I thought I was a pretty good driver. Twenty-five years without a ticket, no accidents—what people commonly refer to as a defensive driver. I had developed safe driving habits that I was eager to pass along to my daughter. But since she began taking driver's ed I found out what a lousy driver I am, at least according to my daughter. It seems that I have developed a lot of unlawful habits that my daughter finds quite infuriating. Whether she is riding shotgun next to me or watching from the backseat, I now have a constant reminder of all the things I am doing wrong.

What is particularly grating is that some of the things she is saying are right. I don't now how to answer her. How do I tell her that it's okay to go a few miles over the speed limit when there are no policemen around? Or that the sign saying "no turn on red" doesn't mean anything at a deserted intersection at 5:30 in the morning? All my life I have encouraged my children to do as I do. But now they are entering my adult world and finding out that what I do is less than perfect. I admit it leaves me feeling a bit uncomfortable.

#24

What do you want your child to be when he or she grows up? Do you have dreams? Does your child know what they are? Does he or she have the same dreams and ambitions or different ones? Write about these questions in your journal.

#25

Does it scare you to think about not having your child go to college until he or she has decided what life work to pursue? Why?

#26

What type of summer work could your child get to begin to explore some of the things he or she enjoys doing? Are you willing to allow this type of exploration if the work doesn't pay well? Are you willing to help in the search for this type of work? If you are, begin brainstorming with your child about the possibilities.

Chapter Nine

Parents of the Future

Preparing Your Children for Life in the Twenty-first Century

Everything that was perceived as my problem as a child has become my career as an adult.

—HOWIE MANDELL

WE ARE PARENTS OF THE future. Kids who are twelve today won't even be out of high school when the 21st century begins. Think things will change much by then?

Absolutely.

Things that are impossible today will be reality sometime next week.

Parenting in the Twenty-first Century

We hardly have time to get to know our children before it's time for them to leave. So how can we, at the same time, get to know a world that doesn't even exist yet? And how in the world can we ever get our apprentice adults ready for it?

Let's take a tour of the very near future to help us realize how unrecognizable the world will be in fifteen years.

Transportation

Your child will go places you never even dreamed of visiting. Just thirty years ago neither I nor any of my friends had traveled even once on an airplane. In contrast, my seven-year-old has traveled ten times by jet. As travel speeds increase and the world seems to shrink, the opportunity to visit remote parts of the globe will give our grown-up children a perception of the world that we will never have.

Communication

Not too many years ago telephones were a luxury. Some of us even had to deal with "party lines" and parents who gave us "just five more minutes" before we had to hang up. Today's children are growing up in a world where the boundaries of interpersonal communication are nearly erased. Advances in communication connect people in ways that are mind-boggling. A few days ago I was outside pulling weeds and had on a tiny headset that was connected to a phone unit with voice-activated dialing. So I simply said, "Larry," and the phone in the house automatically dialed his number. In a matter of seconds, Larry's voice was loud and clear in my ear, and we were talking away while I continued to pull weeds. Can Dick Tracy's wrist picture-phone be far behind?

Computers

You haven't seen the latest computer because it's being released tomorrow. Technology is advancing so rapidly that companies have to hold back new products and plan when to offer them to the public. And each new advance changes the way we live, work, and play.

Already we have hand-held computers that transform scribbled notes into typed text with the push of a button. Soon an audio keyboard will translate spoken words into typewritten text without anyone putting pen to paper. Some schools have already eliminated penmanship in favor of typing classes because writing is becoming an unnecessary skill. In just a few years, typing may not be required either.

Added to this are the endless possibilities afforded by the world-wide computer network, which allows anyone with a computer to have access to any spot on the planet and every bit of human knowledge compiled and assembled.

Education

Between 1900 and 1950 the world's knowledge doubled. And it has doubled again in every decade since 1950! A thirteen-year-old today with average grades knows more than I did when I graduated from college.

So the focus of education is changing from *knowing* information to *getting* information. It is also shifting to earlier discussions of work and career. Everything these days is quicker and more specialized. Liberal arts colleges are dying because they can no longer justify why students should spend four years and $60,000 to get a job that has nothing to do with their degree. Technical institutes are emerging as a logical alternative for people who want to avoid the career confusion plaguing so many college graduates coming out of "old-school" traditions.

We can't even imagine what the school systems will look like for our children's children.

Leisure

Video games didn't even exist fifteen years ago, but today we have "virtual reality." Just put a helmet on your head and step into the world of your video experience. (A scary thought for any parent who has watched a video game for more than ten seconds.) As the time available for leisure activities increases, our children will have to make decisions about time usage that you and I never had to make.

Food

"Eat your vegetables," won't mean much to our grandchildren. Natural ways of eating are working their way back into our diets and improving them. Decisions made at grocery stores in the next century will be very different from the ones **183** we make now. We have discovered more about the relationship between food and health in the last twenty years than we had since people ate grub straight from the ground.

Young adults of the next century will know much more about food than we do, but not because of what they learn in school. Their knowledge will come through the new ways we are being taught (news shows, magazines, newspapers, interpersonal communication).

While some people will always eat what is bad for them, many will be affected by knowledge—just as we've seen happen with smoking in the last few years. Culture demands it, and it will happen.

Medicine

Gall bladder surgery at one time was extremely painful, but it has now been reduced to a non-invasive surgical procedure. A flashlight is inserted through the belly button—Ouch! Still sounds painful to me—and two small incisions are made. A tiny camera goes into one and a tiny instrument for doing the work goes into the other. Remarkable!

Medicine, something that conjures up images of pain for people in our generation and older, will occupy quite a different place in our children's experience. Cancers are being healed in what seems like "Star Trekian" fashion. And dentists are developing new preventative technologies every year. My son is investigating the new surgeries to correct his near-sightedness. And the "miracles" keep coming.

Finances

The average person in the United States eats out, believe it or not, *at least once a day*. My sixteen-year-old son pays more money for one pair of gym shoes than I paid for ten pairs when I was his age. We have more cars, TVs, stereos, clothes, and better homes than we had a generation ago. We have more of everything. And that means our children come "out of the chute" at a different place than we did. Prepare yourself for the fact that your child will have an unusual view of money.

Last week our family was driving home and I commented that it was too bad we didn't have any cash to stop for dinner. Nine-year-old Megan piped up from the back seat, "Why don't we stop at one of those machines that gives you money?"

I asked her if she knew how those machines work (we call them "cash stations" in the Midwest).

"Sure," she said. "You stick a card in and tell it how much money you want, and it gives it to you. Can I get one of those cards, Dad?"

Scary, isn't it?

Is There Anything that *Doesn't* Change?

The best thing to remember in the midst of all this change is that we, the parents, can be the solid ground.

Because this is a fact that's also very true: Even though many things change, many stay the same. It's important for every parent to know the difference between the two.

What are some of those things? I've started a list below. Why don't you finish it to remind yourself of things that never change.

1. Love
2. Truth
3. Laughter
4. Integrity
5.
6.
7.
8.

Family traditions are important. Wise family traditions, that is. In a fast-changing world, children need repeated, time-honored, worthwhile rituals to hold onto. But sometimes we do things just because that's the way we've always done them. Think of two wise traditions in your family. Now think of two things you do simply because your family did them when you were growing up. Do they need an adjustment to make them worthy of your family's time?

Crystal Ball Gazing

If you could stare into the second half of your child's life, you would know how to prepare him or her to soar into the future. But your soon-to-be adult will face situations impossible for you to predict. If we could *s t r e t c h* that imagination

186

of yours, however, maybe we could get some good ideas to use in preparing your almost-adult for the future.

TURN THIS PAGE
TO LOOK INTO THE FUTURE

Notice the changes your daughter is going through. See the difference between the way she looked yesterday and the way she looks today. Now look at your son. If you can get him to stop for a minute, you'll be able to see him grow.

For the next few moments envision what things lay ahead for your children. Your ideas are nothing more than guesses, of course, but the exercise will help you frame how you might use what precious time you have left in the nest.

Listen to your father who gave you life, and do not despise your mother when she is old.
PROVERBS 23:22

What do you see?

The realities of adolescent life are difficult for children to adust to. Considering your child's natural abilities, what two things might he or she have trouble adjusting to as puberty hits and takes control.

1.
2.

Example: *My daughter studies best with someone else. When she gets into high school and her homework takes more time and is more difficult, we won't be able to give her the one-on-one study time she requires. She will have to complete assignments on her own.*

NESTING TIPS

What are you going to do about the points you've listed? Are you going to let them hit you like a ton of bricks? Or are you going to plan ahead? Sometimes planning ahead means being ready to change *yourself*. Are you ready to quit treating your young adult like a child? Doing so may mean letting your son or daughter make decisions that leave you uncomfortable. What adjustments can you make to help your child acquire the skills or understanding to meet these situations successfully?

What do you see?

As children get older, the ongoing series of "First Time Events" gets more serious. The first time your son took a step was cause for a family celebration, but the first time he takes the car is cause for an all-day prayer vigil.

Keeping in mind your child's natural abilities as well as your own, what two responsibilities will be the most difficult for you to hand off?

1.
2.

A good name is more desirable than great riches; to be esteemed is better than silver or gold.
PROVERBS 22:1

Example: *My daughter will soon be deciding what young men to spend time with. Rather than wait around to criticize the guys I perceive to be "wrong choices," I want to help her learn to make good choices.*

NESTING TIPS

These are serious considerations to factor into your flight training schedules concerning this topic. Many of these "first" responsibilities have serious implications if handled improperly. For instance, letting your son have the car keys can kill someone if he is not yet ready to drive.

189

There is a way that seems right to a man, but in the end it leads to death.
PROVERBS 16:25

What do you see?

One day in the not-too-distant future your son will have to provide his own meals, do his own laundry, balance his own checkbook, clean his own bathroom, and wash his own dishes. All by himself.

Right now is a great time to get your child ready for life in the big city.

Knowing what things your child does well naturally, what two things will be the hardest for him or her to do as an adult?

1.
2.

Example: *My daughter does things best when she has a deadline. I am concerned about her taking care of the "regular" responsibilities like paying bills and balancing a checkbook.*

NESTING TIPS

If you make a list of adult "gotta-do's" and teach them to your children early, you will separate them from those who flutter when the reality of living on their own collides with their inability to perform adult responsibilities.

What do you see?

Few children make it through life unscathed. Somehow, either by accident or as a result of their own choices, something bad will happen. They may get kicked out of school, get fired from a job, get left at the altar, or become seriously ill. These things happen to everyone.

Identify two things you believe will be difficult for your child to face.

He who fears the Lord has a refuge.
PROVERBS 14:26

1.
2.

Example: *Death. I want my children to understand the reality of death, and I don't want their first experience to be my demise. I want to be the one to tell them what I believe about eternal life.*

NESTING TIPS

It's sort of like insurance. You hope you don't need it, but you buy it just in case. That's the way it is with preparing your child to face catastrophes.

We have friends who own a funeral home, so we took the kids over one Saturday morning and spent time asking questions and being shown around. Every once in a while we walk through old cemeteries and try to imagine what the families buried there must have been like. Be creative and trust me. Get your insurance.

Who can say,
"I have kept my heart pure"?
PROVERBS 20:9

What do you see?

Some people use the term *blind spots* to describe the black holes of life that people get sucked into. Natural abilities lure children perilously close to the rim of bad decisions, and sometimes they fall into the chasm. By anticipating the "black holes" in your child's future, you can help develop the wisdom needed to step away. Name two "black holes" you see in your child's future.

1.
2.

Example: *My son loves to acquire things. He is always looking for the best deal, and he's always bringing stuff home from other people's garage sales. I want to prepare him for a world of aggressive advertisers who will tempt him to spend his future before he even gets it.*

NESTING TIPS

How many parents have said, after their child has blown it big time, "I've seen it coming since he was six years old." Walk alongside your children through some of those situations now—while you can still hold their hand and guide them. Talk through potential temptations using their natural passion to help you understand it and figure out how to deal with it.

192

What do you see?

In case you haven't noticed, a whole lot of marriages aren't working out these days. You can weave some wonderfully strong fibers into your nest to improve your child's chances of having a successful marriage. Considering the unique child you have been raising, what two things would most affect his or her marriage?

Let love and faithfulness never leave you—write them on the tablet of your heart.
PROVERBS 3:3

1.

2.

Example: *My daughter gets very angry when she doesn't get her own way. She doesn't know how to negotiate, so if she can't have her own way she just gives in. She needs to learn how to work through a discussion to a compromise that works.*

NESTING TIPS

A healthy marriage of your own is the most precious gift you can give your children. What are they learning from your marriage relationship about compromise? About affection? Someday they will develop a marriage from scratch, and what they have learned from your example, even more than what they have learned from everything you have said, will make all the difference in their ability to succeed.

193

Lazy hands make a man poor, but diligent hands bring wealth.
PROVERBS 10:4

What do you see?

What do you see in the work crystal ball? A salesperson? An accountant? A teacher? A carpenter? A writer? A banker? A scientist? What can you do to help your child do even better the things he or she does well naturally? Identify two careers your child might enjoy.

1.
2.

Example: *My daughter loves to teach. Since she was five years old she has arranged her room into a classroom, given tests to her little friends, and graded their papers. We talk a lot about studying to be a teacher.*

NESTING TIPS

The activities that your children will enjoy most as adults are those that enable them to use their natural abilities. My son loves carpentry. I stink at it, so I am always trying to team him up with someone who is good at it. Helping your son start a hobby or finding a mentor for your daughter are responsible ways of preparing your child for a future career.

One Last Word

Take a deep breath. That's a lot of serious looking you've just done.

Do you see how ordinary events in your home today will affect what will happen to your child tomorrow? Looking ahead to next year and the next decade are as much a part of parenting as planning for tomorrow, next week, and next month.

If you plan today with your child's tomorrow in mind, I can promise you one thing: You will see the results . . . tomorrow.

And that is exactly what everything in this book leads to—how to make an impact on the tomorrows of the young adult in your life. It's an opportunity you have for only a short time. Make the most of it.

Coming to the End of Yourself

More light!

—GOETHE'S LAST WORDS

**S**omewhere out there among all the books and discussions about human behavior and raising kids and living as healthy adults is an unspoken ideal: To be the parent of a mature son or daughter.

maturity, *n., slow and careful process of natural growth leading to full development.*

For children to be fully developed (or at least set firmly on the right path) they must realize the enthusiasm of their passion as well as the potential pain that is attached to it. They must have the confidence that emerges from the understanding that what they do best can cause intense pain if they do it at the wrong time or in the wrong place.

Children must come to the end of themselves before they are ready to leave the nest.

Our son, Joshua, is sixteen, and he and I have pounded heads regularly during the past three years as I have tried to set him free to make more of his own decisions. (It's not easy to change from discipline-giver to direction-giver.) The other evening I sat on the edge of his bed to talk about a conflict he was having at school with an individual in a theatrical production.

"Well, Dad," he sighed. "I know what I want to do. But do you think it's the best way to do it?"

I couldn't answer him right away. I was overcome by the sound of the words "but do *you* think . . ." They were music to a father's ears. For at least one moment, Joshua had come to the end of himself. And that, of course, is really the beginning of being himself.

Let the College of Child Development at

FAMILY UNIVERSITY™

bring the wisdom of *Out of the Nest* to your group!

Discovering Your Child's Design is a dynamic four-hour course hosted across America by organizations like yours. The presentation is a fast-paced mix of entertaining lecture with computerized visuals, lots of interactive workshop time and plenty of question and answer interchange. The emphasis is always on the practical application of ideas whether to toddlers or teenagers. Taught live by a Family University Certified Instructor, the course can be styled for fathers only, mothers only, or mixed parenting audiences.

Participants leave with superb take-home resources and a solid grasp of how to apply insights into their child's unique design in areas such as education, motivation, discipline and rewards.

FAMILY UNIVERSITY™ is a "college without walls" curriculum returning strength to America's families by renewing the practical skills and time-honored principles which support successful marriage and family relationships. Courses are hosted by community, corporate and church organizations concerned with the importance of family life.

Other course offerings include: *Secrets of Fast-Track Fathering, Fathering Confidence: Shaping your winning style* and *Saving Your Marriage Before It Starts.*

For more information contact:
Family University™
P.O. Box 500050
San Diego, CA 92150-0050
Voice: (619) 487-7099 • FAX: (619) 487-7356
E-mail: FamilyU@aol.com

The Five Key Habits of Smart Dads
Paul Lewis

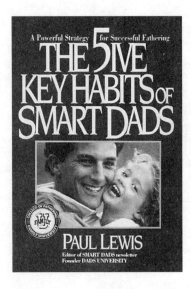

ISBN 0-310-20667-7 Softcover
Price: $12.99

This book inspires fathers and equips them to be more effective. Not a book of rules or impossible goals, *The Five Key Habits of Smart Dads* offers a simple model for effective fathering. Tips, quotes, and activities are provided to help dads offer the most significant gifts children can receive: love and encouragement. A discussion guide is included.

Here's what others are saying:

"This book is pure inspiration. Paul Lewis helped me with practical wisdom and insightful truth. I have used something in this book every day since reading it."

Jim Burns, President
National Institute of Youth Ministry

"Paul Lewis has a knack for offering practical advice in an engaging, often humorous manner."

William R. Mattox, Jr.
Director, Fatherhood Campaign, Family Research Council

"This is a readable, practical book."
Jay Kesler, President, Taylor University, Upland, Indiana

An Audio Pages edition is also available:

ISBN:0-310-61688-3
Price: $14.99

Born to Fly
Thom Black with Lynda Stephenson

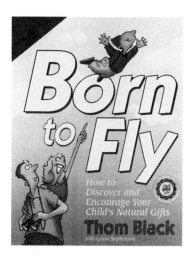

ISBN: 0-310-40281-6 Softcover
Price: $14.99

Raising a child, writes Thom Black, is an art, not a science. Filled with hands-on, practical tips, *Born to Fly* is designed to help you see your child as a unique creation with his or her own set of strengths and weaknesses. Whether your child is a toddler or a teenager, *Born to Fly* will help you identify what your child likes to do best, where your child feels most comfortable, how to reward your child for work well done, and who can help your child excel.

A companion workbook is also available.

ISBN 0-310-40283-2
Price: $5.99